DIY Camper
& RV Reno

First Published in 2025 by Cool Springs Press, an imprint of The Quarto Group,
100 Cummings Center, Suite 265-D, Beverly, MA 01915, USA.
T (978) 282-9590 F (978) 283-2742

Cool Springs Press titles are also available at discount for retail, wholesale, promotional, and bulk purchase. For details, contact the Special Sales Manager by email at specialsales@quarto.com or by mail at The Quarto Group, Attn: Special Sales Manager, 100 Cummings Center, Suite 265-D, Beverly, MA 01915, USA.

29 28 27 26 25   1 2 3 4 5

ISBN: 978-0-7603-9240-9

Digital edition published in 2025
eISBN: 978-0-7603-9241-6

Library of Congress Cataloging-in-Publication Data is available.

Design and page layout: Megan Jones Design
Photography: All photos by Chadwick Payne except Nate Kantor & Garrett Foster Green with nomaticana on pages 4, 62 (both); Sefra Escobar on pages 6, 7, 66, 105 (middle right, bottom), 125, 155 (bottom), 158 (right), 159 (bottom right), 163 (bottom), 167 (bottom), 181 (bottom right), 186, 190; Shutterstock on pages 20, 22, 27, 29, 72, 85 (both), 110 (all except bottom right), 111 (top), 134 (bottom), 144 (both), 148 (top left); The Bay-Browns (@BBandtheRV) on page 65 (all); Allison Lundee (@proverbs31girl) on page 64 (both); Elijah & Leann Dixon (@fivetalentshomes) on page 67; Brad & Renee Lois with WiscoFlip on page 68; Dan Waitkus and Samantha Serfilippi on page 69 (all except top); Heather McQueen (@forgeandtrek) on page 69 (top)
Illustration: Shutterstock

Printed in China

DIY Camper & RV Reno

Restoring and
Designing Vintage,
Retro, and Classic
Trailers and RVs with
Nailgun Nelly

JANELLE AND CHADWICK PAYNE

COOL
SPRINGS
PRESS

contents

Introduction

Welcome! My name is Janelle, but most people know me as Nailgun Nelly! You can always find me building something on our property here on the beautiful central coast of California. I have always had a passion to create unique and fun spaces. Even as a child, I would talk my mom into taking me to the local hardware store so I could build my own four-poster bed out of PVC pipe and design my room with different "themes."

As luck would have it, I married the love of my life, Chadwick, a fellow critical care nurse, who also shared the same affinity for building on a budget. We ended up remodeling two homes and shortly after were blessed with two boys. I then scaled back and focused on being part-time at the hospital and a stay-at-home mom. And just like that, I had more time to focus on my true passion, building and designing (with my two boys in tow).

Fast forward a few more years: Chad and I built a chic studio apartment to house fellow travel nurses when our community was devastated by COVID-19. From those tough times, we fell in love with building and designing small spaces. You guessed it—that's where our love for restoring retro travel trailers came from. Since then, we have renovated numerous vintage trailers and even built out a camper van that our little family called home as we drove across the gorgeous Southwest US. From stationary tiny homes to off-grid rigs, we have slowly become experts for anything trailer/tiny home–related.

If you have ever dreamed of restoring a vintage travel trailer, you will find that it is more than a renovation project; it's a journey back in time infused with creativity and craftsmanship. Throughout the process of stripping down its worn surfaces, you are bound to think you are "in too deep!" But with the help of the many tutorials, I hope this book will be a great resource to give you the confidence to tackle anything that may come your way. I promise an extremely rewarding outcome is at the end of this journey. With attention to detail in every fixture and finish, from customized appliances to retro furnishings, your trailer will transform into a timeless retreat on wheels.

In the end, as you tow it onto open roads, your restored gem will not only fulfill dreams of adventure but also preserve a piece of cultural history, offering a second life that honors its storied past. Let this book be your guide through this process. These renovations will take a little elbow grease and try your resilience. Due to the nature of these trailers and RVs, the chances your projects can look exactly like the ones in these pages are slim. However, that's what makes any adventure worthwhile! This book provides the foundation of ideas and techniques. You can, and should, make it yours! So go ahead, turn the page, and join me for the adventure of a lifetime.

—Janelle (and Chadwick) Payne

finding the perfect travel trailer

In a world of sleek, modern campers and high-tech recreational vehicles (RVs), there is something enchanting about the charm and nostalgia that a vintage trailer brings. These quaint relics of a bygone era hold stories and memories of countless adventures. They also offer a unique canvas for creativity and restoration, which is why I am thrilled to reveal my secrets for breathing new life into not only vintage trailers, but all RVs as well.

Our 1970 Ideal the day we brought her home, pre-renovation

My journey into the world of trailer restoration began when I stumbled upon a dusty, neglected gem hiding in a forgotten corner of a neighbor's property. It was a vintage trailer from the 1970s. Its aluminum shell, though covered in moss, glistened with potential and the promise of a glorious revival. It was love at first sight, and I could not resist the idea of giving this trailer a new lease on life.

Prior to obtaining our first trailer, Chad and I had just finished building an almost 400 square foot (37 square meter) studio. During that time, we fell in love with designing small spaces. Unlike our primary home, where every design decision you must live with, there is something freeing that comes with designing a tiny home, allowing you to be as conservative or bold, trendy, or timeless as you desire in a space all its own. So, it was during the start of the pandemic of 2020 when acquiring a travel trailer to design was a no-brainer. Not only could I continue to explore this passion, but we could take our little family on amazing adventures once it was completed. Little did I

know how popular it would be with my social media audience, and who would have known that we would end up writing a book in the process! I will say we did come across our first trailer by chance as it was in our neighbor's yard, and she wanted to get rid of it. This made for a perfect trial run since we did not invest money into buying it. Since that first renovation, Chad and I have learned many things in the process of acquiring an RV if you are not fortunate enough to have one given to you. The first and most critical step in renovating an RV is finding the perfect one. It is a

decision that will set the stage for your entire renovation adventure, shaping the space in which you will create memories and write new stories. The right RV will not only cater to your specific needs and desires but also serve as a canvas for your creativity and vision. Everybody will have different needs for what they want in their RV, but the process of searching for the right one is the same. So, let's embark on this chapter's exploration together, as we navigate the landscape of RV options, considerations, the buying process, and tips to uncover the ideal camper for you.

Figuring Out Your Needs

When it comes to picking the perfect RV, there are several key factors and a wide range of options to consider that may or may not suit your family's needs. When Chad and I bought our first camper, and after our first trip, it was clear that the layout was not ideal. When most people ask me what type of camper they should buy, I always recommend renting one. You can rent travel trailers on sites such as RVshare. You quickly know what the camper is missing or if it is more than you need. But most people do not want to deal with the hassle and prefer to take the plunge without any experience. Because of this, let's talk about how you can find your ideal camper the first time.

First, think about the length of the RV. The size you choose will affect its maneuverability, parking options, and ease of towing. Chad and I always lean toward minimalism. We prefer to tow a camper that is just big enough to accommodate our family. When you pick a camper that is on the smaller end overall, the camper will be lighter. The lighter the camper, the easier it is for your vehicle to tow. Most vehicles don't focus on towing ability, but many can do the job. If you are not sure how much your vehicle can tow, give it a quick internet search. The key words to search are *towing capacity*. The towing capacity number represents the maximum towing ability of your vehicle. Once you have this number, simply buy a camper that is under this amount when all the tanks (water, propane, gray, and black) are full. Most campers list their dry weight, but when the freshwater and gray and black tanks are full, this can add several hundred pounds

(over 350 kilograms) of weight. Because of this, we like to stay 20 percent or more under our vehicle's towing capacity. Your car will thank you for this. But most families choose a truck to do the job. If you have a ¾-ton (3,856 to 4,536 kg) truck, you will be able to tow about anything! These trucks can pull upward to 18,000 pounds (8,165 kg). To give you an idea, our 16-foot (4.9 m) 1964 Prowler weighs in just under 4,000 pounds (1,814 kg).

Speaking of camper length, do you want one or two axles? If you decide to buy a trailer less than 20 feet (6.1 m) in length, you may notice there is only one axle. Why does this matter? Chad and I really do not enjoy hauling around a heavy camper, preferring to sacrifice a spacious interior for an easy towing experience. However, when we acquired our 1970

›› Our first family trailer that we renovated

A 24-foot (7.3 m) two-axel trailer

Prowler, a 16-foot (4.9 m) trailer with one axle, we noticed that it was a little bouncy, and if the interior weight were not distributed equally when packing, the trailer would feel like it was swerving a little bit, leading to an overall nerve-racking towing experience. This is common with single axles, and that is why we now prefer to have a trailer that is still on the smaller end but has two axles. The towing experience is so much better! Still, antisway bars are available to keep your trailer in line with your vehicle. These are basically modified hitches that utilize steel bars that attach to the frame of the trailer. A quick installation for a much better tow is just another thing to consider when on the hunt.

Another consideration is the style of sleeping arrangements that is important to you. Whether you are a couple, a family, or a group of friends, the number of beds, and whether they require work to set up, might make or break your love for your camper. Check out the various bed options available in different

campers. We have two young boys, so campers that have built-in bunk beds are superconvenient. As for us, we prefer a bed that is always ready to go. Our camper van had a dedicated bed. When we were ready to go to bed, we just had to hop in, and when we woke, it did not require us to put it away to make the space functional. I say this because our current camper's bed is a couch during the day. At night, we pull it out, and it takes up most of the kitchen when in this position. So, in the morning, we cannot simply roll out of bed and make coffee. If I am required to do anything other than breathe prior to having my first cup of coffee, my day is almost unsalvageable. I would love to say I'm joking, but Chad knows how I like to start my day, so he makes sure to get our space set up right away. Additionally, our couch cushions double as a bed mattress. They do the job, but obviously, a real mattress will result in a more restful night, and poor Chad is getting old! His old bones are very

A 16-foot (4.9 m) single-axel trailer

particular about where they rest. So, the main points to consider are do you want a stationery or convertible bed? Are you okay with 4-inch (10.2 cm)-thick bench cushions that turn into your sleeping area or would you prefer a nice thick mattress? And how many sleeping areas do you need? Once you have these specifics nailed down, keep them in mind as you search.

Camping is all about making memories through adventure. Some people like to just get away from their home, pull into a campsite, and plug in. This type of camping can be great, and many RV resorts have some serious luxuries: pools, restaurants, and parks. Getting a little taste of adventure all while enjoying resort perks is awesome but is that really camping? I say yes, but I do enjoy a real adventure as well.

◄◄ Many older RVs have upper bunks like this that can be folded up when not in use.

Chad, the boys, and I fell in love with off-grid camping. Off-grid camping essentially means that there is no water, sewage, or electricity for you. Everything you need to enjoy yourself you are required to bring. Trailers have large freshwater tanks for drinking and bathing and gray and black tanks to hold gray water and sewage. But what about electricity? A camper equipped with a couple of solar panels and a battery bank will allow you to go off the grid and truly experience camping. If this is something that interests you, and if you don't want to install the system yourself, make sure the camper you purchase has an off-grid system installed. Often, you will not find a trailer with a nice off-grid system, and you will need to install it yourself. There is a section about electrical in chapter 2 that describes in detail how to know what to purchase and how to install a custom off-grid system if you would like to explore this.

Front of a rigid solar panel

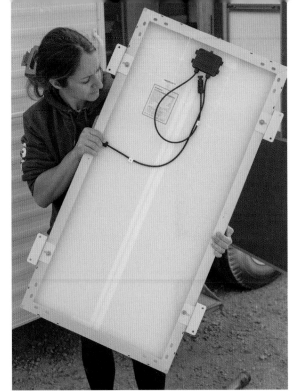

Back of a rigid solar panel

Chad and I have found that most vintage trailers do not have an awning. An awning extends and retracts, creating a shaded area that is also useful when it rains. More than the protection from the elements, this awning creates a finished feeling to your outdoor space, comparable to a fence in your backyard. If you can find a trailer with an awning, it will be as old as the trailer itself, and because of this, the fabric will need to be replaced. If no awning mechanism is on the trailer, they can easily be purchased and installed. Another common awning on vintage trailers is found in the front, covering the large window. If you find a trailer missing this piece, it is next to impossible to find a replacement, so I always make sure the fold-down awning is there.

Since you have decided that a vintage travel trailer is right for you, it is important to know some features that newer ones just do better. New travel trailers have slide-outs. These sections extend out, creating a much larger living space. I haven't met a person who doesn't like more open living space, so I will say that

vintage campers are deficient in this category. Another antiquated feature in vintage campers is their insulation, or lack thereof. If you live in a cold environment, just know that the inside will be the same temperature as the outside. If you are at a campsite with shore power (a place to plug in), you will be able to run heaters. But, if you plan to camp off the grid, make sure to dress warm! But there *is* something that the old trailers have on the new. As the saying goes, "They just don't make them like they used to." Sorry to be corny, but a vintage travel trailer's aluminum siding will last a lifetime. This is why you see so many Airstreams still on the road today. Aluminum can always be refinished and does not rust. Unfortunately for recent trailers, their fiberglass exterior quickly loses its sheen when sitting in the sun, and water intrusion will lead to delamination, where the siding bubbles out. So as with all things, consider the pros and cons.

➤ An original awning with wood accent added

Where Do You Look, and How Do You Approach the Purchase?

So, you want to find the perfect retro travel trailer to restore, but where do you find one? Luckily, there are several options, and you will no doubt find the trailer for you. The main thing is to be patient and know that you will eventually come across a keeper!

RV dealerships are the most mainstream way to find a travel trailer, but you will not find many deals with this route, and they rarely, if at all, stock vintage models. Additionally, you will pay above market value. The salespeople here are trained to make you fall in love with whatever they have on site, and you will be paying a premium for the convenience they can provide. But it is never a bad idea to talk to a sales rep at one of these locations, let them know what you are looking for, and have them reach out to you if they come across what you are looking for.

Your best search tool though is the internet. Several websites specialize in retro camper sales. Not only can you find thousands of listings for sale, but you also can refine your search to locate exactly what you are looking for. You will be able to use these website's search engines to filter a specific year, make, and model. Here, you will find trailers that are being sold by a dealership and by the owners themselves. For example, the website airstreammarketplace.com caters to Airstream enthusiasts, while vintagecampertrailers.com has a variety of retro trailers to choose from.

Believe me, if you are patient and willing to travel, perhaps even out of state, you will find the perfect camper for you. Most sellers who utilize a professional selling website know what they have and have already done most of the restoring. They know the value, and they know an enthusiast out there is willing to pay a premium for their vintage camper.

This next method is by far my favorite and where we've had the most luck finding the best deals. Facebook Marketplace lets people sell just about anything. You will find several local campers for sale in your area. Marketplace's search engine is very effective, and it learns to know what you like, showing you more campers as they are listed. If you don't have a Facebook account, I recommend that you get one just to access this feature. People will make a profile simply to utilize Facebook Marketplace to buy and sell just about anything. It is essentially a 24/7 garage sale! Most people who sell on Marketplace don't know what they have, or they don't want to pay a professional website to make a listing. This makes Facebook Marketplace an ideal arena to find an amazing deal. Recently, Chad and I purchased the 1970 Ideal displayed in this book through Marketplace. We bought it for $2,000 USD.

One more effective method is word of mouth or just knocking on a door with a trailer in the driveway. Let your friends and family know that you're in the market. Make a post on social media. You will again be surprised by how many people have trailers they want to get rid of, but they never took the time to make a listing. We actually acquired two retro travel trailers with this method, both for free. One we restored for $5,000 USD, and we currently rent it out as a tiny home for traveling nurses and doctors. As for the other, we restored it for $11,000 USD and use it as our family travel trailer. We also bought a 2015 Ford Transit for $25,000 USD, turned it into a camper van for $15,000 USD, and sold it for

Our completely renovated 1970 Ideal travel trailer

$70,000 USD. This obviously helps with your budget and gives you a lot more financial flexibility when restoring your gem. So, speaking of deals, let's talk about how to go about purchasing a camper you have found.

BUYER BEWARE: QUESTIONS TO ASK BEFORE VIEWING

So, you found the perfect camper and have arranged a viewing. From severe water damage to broken windows, let's make sure you know what's considered a deal-breaker.

When people make listings to sell a vintage camper, they like to fluff the listing. You'll find that all the good things are spoken about and none of the bad. A lot of times it is because the seller isn't even aware of the issues. For instance, several years back we were looking for a toy hauler. Everything in the listing looked great, but when Chad crawled on the roof to look for leaks, there was a big hole. When we walked in, the damage was masked by a cabinet in the kitchen, which was not easy to find. The amount of damage on this newer trailer would have cost a lot of time and money, making the asking price too high, but more so, we didn't want the headache of fixing the issue. Nevertheless, when purchasing a retro camper, you will find some water intrusion, so make sure that the damage isn't too extensive. In chapter 2 we will go more in depth with water damage.

Like I mentioned, sellers like to hype their listing, and they always seem to miss the giant dent in the aluminum siding when posting photos. Recently, we went to view a trailer, and the back side of the trailer had a huge hole. "Hmm, I never even noticed that," the owner said. If a dent is large or there are big holes and you are not an auto body fabricator, just move onto the next trailer. Replacing the siding is

Keep in mind what climates will you be taking your trailer to.

Replacing vintage windows can be pricey! We only pick trailers with windows intact.

not only going to cost a lot, but finding the siding that matches your current trailer is going to be an ordeal. Small holes are a different story. They do make several aluminum hole fillers, so some repairs are fairly simple, but I tend to stray away from the larger exterior body work that may need to be repaired.

Ensuring that the seller has a title under their name is important too. You would be surprised by how many people acquire an old camper from someone without a title and then want to sell it to someone else. This is illegal. If you purchase a camper without a title and then take it to the DMV, they will ask that you have the sheriff's department run its VIN number. If the camper has been reported stolen, guess what? They will arrest you! Simply have the seller do this for you. If they want to

make the sale, they need to get the paperwork proving it is in fact theirs to sell.

A vintage camper that has been sitting in someone's yard for a decade undoubtedly needs new tires. Some are not in the worst condition. You may be able to bring an air compressor for a short trip down the road if you are close to home or if they are in decent enough shape, a quick drive to the closest tire shop. They will be happy to place new trailer tires on. But if you need to get on a highway or travel long distances, be prepared to change the tires out on site before driving away with the unit.

You will never truly know what the electrical situation is until you open the walls up, but if the trailer is old enough, aluminum wiring was used before copper. If your camper has aluminum wiring, you may need to change all the wires out for new ones. Aluminum is much more fragile and can break. This is an easy task overall, and we will cover this in the electrical section, but it is something to consider.

Make sure the repairs that must be completed are in your budget, or at least, you should know how much they will cost. For example, many of these retro campers have broken windows. This repair alone could make or break your budget as vintage trailer windows are difficult to acquire. Another example would be a subfloor that needs to be completely changed. Most have small sections of subfloor with an issue that needs repair, but removing an entire subfloor means the whole trailer will need to be gutted and that can certainly be a huge deal-breaker.

THE PITCH AND VIEWING

Someone is always looking to make a quick sale, and like they say, one man's trash is another man's treasure. It really is wild how many people have an old camper sitting in their backyard. Most had dreams just like you to revitalize the relic and give it a second chance at life. Hopefully, unlike you, most found that they were just too busy or unwilling to learn the skills to bring this dream to fruition. Then, they list the camper, hoping to get market value, but soon find out that there are few bites. Those who do come to look can't see past the bugs, moss, and dirt, ultimately leaving the negotiation without making an offer. As the weeks go by, the seller gets frustrated. They just want to make the sale and free up space on their property. This is where you come in, confident and ready to wheel and deal. Armed with the art of negotiation, you look at the camper, unimpressed, skeptical, and seem genuinely uninterested. But you like the trailer, it's everything you want, all your boxes are checked, and any potential deal-breakers are addressed. As you continue

your act, you decide to make an offer, and because you arrived with cash in hand, this is going to be a sure deal. You offer far below the listed price and tell them you can drive away with the trailer today. For most, especially if the camper has been listed for some time, it is an offer they cannot refuse and an end to their headache. For example, we purchased a toy hauler with this method. The seller wanted $15,000 USD, so we showed up with $10,000 USD and said we could take it today. This seller was actually moving to another state soon, so they needed the trailer gone. You guessed it—they took $10,000 USD. We put a couple thousand into this project and sold it for a $10,000 USD profit.

Another important task to do is to research what similar trailers are going for prior to making an offer, both in their distressed state and when restored. You do not want to acquire a camper that needs to be restored for $5,000 USD, put $10,000 USD into restoring it, and later come to find out it is only worth $8,000 USD. Chad and I always find a deal because of this. When you know you have equity in your trailer, there is less financial stress on your shoulders when restoring and designing. Knowing you always can sell for profit makes the entire process much more enjoyable. So, take your time and make sure you get a fair price. This is another reason to stay patient. The right trailer will show up if you are persistent enough.

The point I am trying to make here is to always look for a deal. Travel trailers are a dime a dozen, and someone is always looking to sell. If the current trailer's seller is unwilling to budge on the price, don't sweat it. Some folks have an emotional attachment to the camper and hold its value too high. If this is the case, just tell them thank you for allowing you to view it and move onto the next. Keep an eye on the listing, and if it still has not sold after some time, reach back out and see if the seller has reconsidered. As they say, patience is a virtue.

going through systems

___

When taking on a fixer-upper, you will need supplies. Because of this, you will get to know your local hardware store very well. For the restoration, you will find most of your items here, but when designing your camper, you may want something with a custom touch. For this, online specialty stores are a great option. Several websites exclusively sell RV and camper supplies. On these online sites, such as RecPro or etrailer, you will find absolutely everything you need to complete the job. Of these online websites, some carry vintage supplies only. So, with these options, you will always be able to find what you need. For the design portion of your renovation, the sky's the limit. If you can imagine it, you can utilize it in your design. We will touch on this later in the book.

Electrical

Your three main resources when camping are propane, water, and electricity, with the latter having the most flexibility for a creative design. When brainstorming your electrical system, you should keep in mind what your goals for camping are. Where do you see your adventures taking you? Will you find yourself at luxurious RV resorts or does a secluded Bureau of Land Management (BLM) parking spot next to the Grand Canyon pique your interest? Or maybe a mix of the two?

Chad and I fell in love with off-grid camping when we embarked on a month-long trip in our camper van that had a 200Ah lithium battery bank, a 2,000-watt inverter, and three different methods to charge our system. This allowed us to go about anywhere our tires would take us. Still, as much as we love off-grid adventures, there is a good chance you can find us at luxurious RV resorts during the summer, hanging by the poolside. Some of the battery lingo I mentioned may seem like jargon, but I will describe in detail everything you need to know to design the perfect system to fit your needs, allowing you to embark on any journey your heart desires.

It is important to quickly talk about the two types of voltages in your camper. Just like your home, your camper will have 120-volt receptacles throughout, and some of your appliances will be powered by 120 volts as well. The other voltage is 12 volts. This is supplied by your onboard battery, and this will also power appliances and let you charge certain devices. Interestingly, some appliances can run off both 120V and 12V. Most camper trailers and RVs have an in-line AC-to-DC converter, changing the supply from 120V to 12V.

Let's first discuss the term *shore power*. This means that you intend to pull into a camping spot that allows you to hook up to water, sewage, and electricity. Your camper will have a similar electrical setup to your home: a power line running into your camper through a breaker box and AC plugs. A shore power line will supply power not from a battery in your rig, but by plugging into the campsite power source. You will be able to power heaters, air conditioners, and have all the essentials easily accessible.

Often, when you purchase a vintage camper, it will come equipped with shore power hookup, but it will likely be outdated. For safety, you should update the system.

First, your power cord that plugs into the campsite post must be changed. You will have to decide what you will be powering and then choose the appropriate cord size: 30A or 50A. Both cables deliver 120 volts, but the amperage is the difference. New campers come standard with a 50A cable, while older rigs were fitted with a 30A cable. The 50A cable will be able to power more appliances than a 30A cable. If your camper is on the larger side and you will be powering an air conditioner or two or more than five circuits, I recommend a 50A cable. If you have a smaller rig and you only have 12-volt ventilation fans and a few AC lights, a 30A cord will suffice.

The cord makes its way into the camper through a main breaker to a converter that routes the electricity to the onboard breaker box. You are going to want to install a new box and breakers. Breakers shut the power off to the appliance if an overload occurs and can be reset, unlike fuses. For every circuit, wires run from the breakers to outlets, fixtures, or appliances. In a camper, many circuits just power one appliance or fixture, although the breaker may be able to handle the load of multiple outlets, depending on what you plug into them. If the wires are copper and the sheaths

⇒ Example of an electrical setup for an off-grid RV

charger

- mains on
- bulk
- absorption
- float

inverter

- inverter on
- overload
- low battery
- temperature

on
off
charger only

- battery charger
- powerassist
- sinewave inverter
- parallel connectable
- transfer switch
- three phase connectable

12.8V 100AH

Rope chandelier light

Finally, the primary breaker panel is wired to an AC-to-DC converter. This awesome device converts 120 volts to 12 volts and allows you to charge your onboard battery that powers all your DC appliances and charging needs. Below, I will go over the simple steps to upgrade your shore power system, and I will make sure to keep it as budget friendly as possible.

Our favorite staycation campsite is located near Pismo Beach, here in California. The area is beautiful: eucalyptus trees, a cute creek, and, of course, the ocean. This little gem has everything, except its dry camping. Dry camping is when the campsite offers you a parking spot and a fire pit if you are lucky. So, you will need to utilize your black and gray tanks' capacity, use your freshwater tanks, and supply your own electricity.

Most campers will have an onboard 12-volt deep cycle battery, and if fully charged, you will use it to power small appliances for a couple days. For us, this just is not good enough. We love our shorter camping trips, but when we really want to get away for several days, we need a way to keep our battery charged. Here you have two options: You can install a larger battery bank or opt to install enough solar power to keep the single battery charged.

Not only is it empowering to know that you can live self-sustained off grid, but it is economical and an easy setup. Before we go over the steps to install your system, let's talk about the type of battery to install, how big of a battery bank you will need and the solar panels you will need. We always install a lithium deep cycle battery. Not only can these batteries be completely discharged without damaging the battery, but they also have many more charge cycles, leading to a longer life. A little math will help you know how big of a bank you will need. Each appliance in your camper has a label listing how many amps and watts it uses per hour. For example, your fridge may use 10 amps

are still in good condition, you will not need to change them. Many older trailers may contain aluminum wiring; this should be replaced as a safety measure.

When purchasing your camper, it's important to analyze the current wires so you can avoid tearing every wall down to install new wires throughout your camper. A wiring diagram is handy for this if one exists. If not, thinking through your system and drawing a basic diagram can provide a great roadmap for the work.

per hour and your ceiling fan uses 5 amps per hour. That is a total of 15 amps per hour. If you have one lithium battery that has a capacity of 100-amp hours, you would only be able to run these two appliances for just over six hours. When we add the appropriate number of solar panels, you can charge the battery with more amps than you are using. Several solar panel calculators online will allow you to input what you use while camping and how many panels you need to offset your usage. Let's talk more about this and discuss the steps to install your electrical set.

I mentioned that we had three ways to charge our battery (a fourth way would be a gas-powered generator). I discussed shore power and solar power earlier. The third method is DC-to-DC charging. Basically, you will use your truck's engine to charge your camper battery while driving, in the same way that the engine charges the truck's battery through the alternator. Most newer vehicles have this ability, and the seven-prong plug that connects your camper to your truck will supply this charging ability to your onboard battery. This is a great way to keep your charge up when you are stopping at multiple campsites on a long trip. But if you plan to set up camp and be stationary for a long period of time, this method wouldn't do you much good. Whereas, when we drove for a month straight across Arizona, Utah, and Nevada, our DC-to-DC charging method was very effective. In fact, some full-time van lifers do not even have solar panels, relying completely on their alternator to keep their battery bank charged.

It is always best to install your electrical system after the interior demo, but before installing aesthetic features. Ensure that your camper is unplugged when working on electrical and that the breakers are in the off position.

camper solar panels

There are two types of solar panels: rigid and flexible. Rigid panels have been around much longer, are very durable, and cost much less. Rigid solar panels do weigh more, have a larger profile, and require the installer to fasten the panel to the roof with screws. Flexible panels are much newer and can be glued to the surface, and their slim profile makes them hardly noticeable. The con to flexible panels is that they do cost more.

HOW TO WIRE A CAMPER TRAILER

Materials and Tools

▷ **Crimp connector kit (with connectors and crimper tool)**
▷ **Heat shrink wire connectors**
▷ **Heat gun**
▷ **Electrical tape**
▷ **14/2 Romex wire**
▷ **6 AWG (American Wire Gauge) wire**
▷ **AC-to-DC converter**
▷ **Fuse box**
▷ **Lithium battery**
▷ **Battery monitor**
▷ **30A or 50A power cord**
▷ **Breaker box and breakers**
▷ **Receptacles and light switches**
▷ **7-prong plug**
▷ **Electric breaker box**
▷ **Multitool wire stripper/crimper**
▷ **Cable or wire clamps**

Instructions

1. Diagram your circuits. A basic wiring diagram does not need to be pretty. It just needs to be clear, so that you see where each element is wired into the system. You also can use this to check your math and make sure you are not overloading any one circuit.

2. Determine which power cord you will use for your shore power system—30A or 50A. (A 30A cord will be fine for a smaller trailer with vent fans, but a 50A cord will work better for a larger trailer and any with an air-conditioning unit.)

3. Run the plug cord through the existing access door, where the cable being replaced is housed, and wire the plug to the breaker box by stripping the ends of the wires coming out of the cords. A 30A cord will be wired with the hot to the main breaker bus bar and neutral and ground to the respective bus bars. A 50A cord will be wired with hot 1 (usually black) connected to one main bus bar, feeding a group of circuits, and hot 2 (usually red) to another main bus bar, feeding a separate group of circuits. Neutral and ground will be wired to their respective bus bars.

Note: Although wire nuts are used to make most wiring connections in a home, the vibration of a camper or RV means the connections are more likely to come apart. That is why it is smart to use crimp connectors with eyelets for terminal connectors and heat shrink wire connectors for the exposed wire ends. To make connections, make sure you have more wire than you need (in case you mess up and must cut off the end). Strip sheathing off the end of the wire to match the length of the crimp-fitting barrel. Slip the end into the connector barrel so that the insulation contacts the end of the barrel. Use the matching crimper slot to crimp the barrel tightly, securing the wire in place. Check the connection to ensure that the fitting is not damaged. If using a heat shrink wire connector, use a heat gun all around the connector barrel until it shrinks and the wire is secured tightly in place.

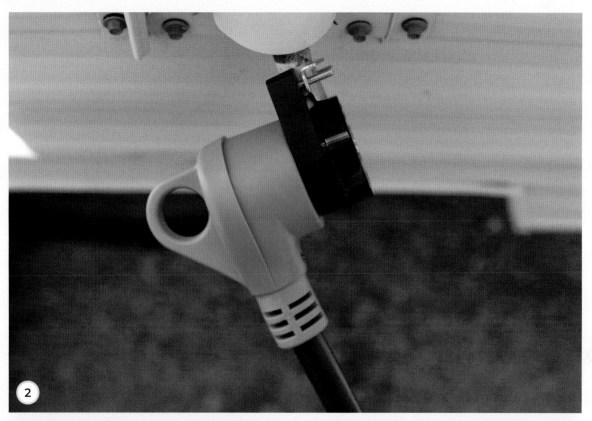

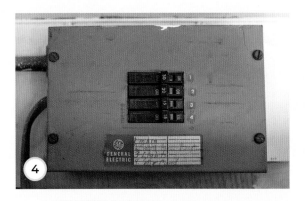

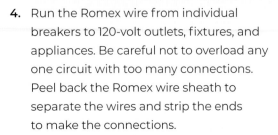

4. Run the Romex wire from individual breakers to 120-volt outlets, fixtures, and appliances. Be careful not to overload any one circuit with too many connections. Peel back the Romex wire sheath to separate the wires and strip the ends to make the connections.

   Note: I use Romex wire—in which the wires for the circuit are molded together; some people prefer to use stranded (single) wiring, which can make it easier to fix a problem or a break in an individual wire.

5. Your AC-to-DC converter will plug into one of the outlets that you installed. (My converter is a RecPro.) The converter is in-line to the DC side of the system (converting shore power AC 120V to DC 12V for battery charging and powering 12-volt fixtures). In some systems, the converter is wired through a breaker box. I wired mine using a 6 AWG wire (6-gauge) to the onboard battery's positive and negative terminals and a ground to the trailer chassis. That way, we charge the onboard battery anytime we are connected to shore power.

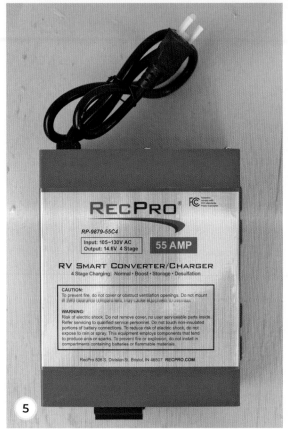

HOW TO INSTALL A SOLAR SYSTEM IN AN RV OR CAMPER TRAILER

Materials and Tools

▷ 14/2 Romex wire
▷ Rigid solar panels and mounting kit
▷ Butyl tape
▷ Self-leveling lap sealant
▷ Multipurpose tool
▷ Caulk gun
▷ Weatherproof silicone sealant
▷ MPPT (Maximum Power Point Tracking) charge controller
▷ Ladder
▷ Heavy-duty work gloves
▷ Tape measure
▷ Sharpie
▷ Multimeter or voltmeter
▷ Power drill and bits
▷ Painter's tape
▷ Zip ties
▷ Cable or wire clamps
▷ Heat shrink wire connectors
▷ Wire cutters
▷ Box wrench
▷ Running lights
▷ Brake lights/taillights

Instructions

1. Plan the panel locations on the camper roof, keeping panels out of the shade from other roof fixtures. Keep panel feet away from edges to avoid compromising the roof's edge seal. Determine the most direct route for the system cables down through the roof. Measure and mark exact locations with the Sharpie.

2. Check the panels and hardware to ensure everything you need for installation has been supplied by the manufacturer. Make sure you have the appropriate lengths of coil and all the tools you will need. It is wise to stage tools and supplies on a tarp on the ground to prevent anything falling off the roof and to keep the project organized.

3. Use the multimeter (or a voltmeter) to check the voltage from the solar panels and ensure they have not been damaged.

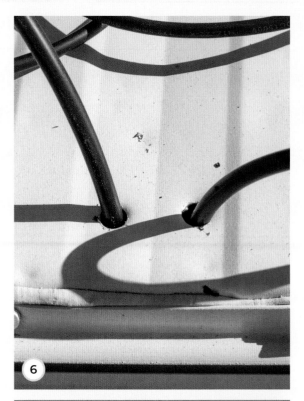

4. Attach the Z bracket feet to the panels. Put the panels in position as planned and mark the screw holes for the Z brackets on the roof with a Sharpie. Mark the hole for the cable to route down into the interior through the roof.

5. Drill the holes for the feet and dab silicone sealant in each screw hole. Line the feet with butyl tape and fasten the feet to the roof. Coat each foot in a liberal covering of self-leveling lap sealant.

6. Drill the hole for the power cables to route down to the controller and battery compartment. Mark each end of the positive cable with painter's tape and feed the cables down through the hole. Route the cables to the controller and battery compartment, using zip ties and cable clamps to keep them orderly and secure.

7. Fasten the controller to the battery compartment wall with the supplied hardware. Connect the panel cable to the controller inputs and connect the cables from the controller to the batteries. Keep in mind the shorter the length of wire and the heavier the gauge, the more efficient the charging and less electrical loss you will experience.

   Optional: If your controller includes a meter with readout, run a cable from the controller to the nearest location inside the camper where you can mount the meter and drill an access hole. Mount the meter and connect it to the controller.

8. I connected a battery monitor to the positive and negative battery terminals. Depending on the monitor you buy, it will tell you charge percentage and voltage. (I prefer to monitor the voltage.) Get to know your battery's voltage curve. I use lithium batteries. I can look at the battery's voltage and know how much battery charge we must work with.

9. Connect the panels in series, following the manufacturer's instructions. (It is best to keep the panels covered throughout this process to prevent them from generating voltage. Remove the coverings when you have made all the power cable connections.) Check the controller to ensure current is flowing from the panels and through to the batteries.

10. Tape down the rooftop cables with butyl tape and coat cable entry points in the roof with weatherproof sealant.

11. Run hot and neutral wires from the battery to the DC fuse box. Wire circuits from the breaker to the DC appliances or fixtures. Use the gauge wires recommended by the manufacturer (12-gauge is common). I use a fuse box with at least six slots, and I hook up my fridge, stove, water pump, water heater, lights, and fan.

12. Your retro RV may have an outdated plug for the connection to the tow vehicle. Purchase a seven-prong plug to allow the tow vehicle's battery to power clearance lights, brake lights, and turn signals. Securely mount the wire box for the new plug on the tongue of the hitch and use eyelets and heat shrink wire connectors to prepare wires from the brakes and lights to connect to the appropriate 7 prong plug terminals. Once connected, test all the lights and the brakes before closing up the wire box.

Optional: Replace the clearance lights. (I buy my clearance lights from Amazon.) Replace weathered clearance lights with clean, clear new ones. Connect the positive wire to the trailer's wire and the negative to the frame of the trailer. Lay a bead of weatherproof exterior silicone caulk around the light housing for a leakproof seal.

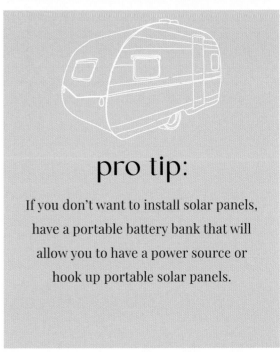

pro tip:

If you don't want to install solar panels, have a portable battery bank that will allow you to have a power source or hook up portable solar panels.

Plumbing

Water is obviously a main resource for you and your family while camping. When you are at a campsite with hookups, all you do is connect a hose that pressurizes your system. But what do you do if you are dry camping? Trailers are equipped with freshwater tanks that provide water for your trip. There are varying sizes to match your needs, but we always like to install the largest tank our camper can hold. Between showers, cooking, and toilets, you would be surprised how quickly 20 gallons (75.7 L) of water will be used.

Because we always can recharge our batteries with solar, and propane goes so far, water always has been our most precious resource when on the road. Still, to our surprise, you will always find potable water in state parks, making refilling your tank simple. Additionally, most dump stations have a refill station, but there is something that turns me off from filling my freshwater tank next to a sewage dump station.

So, you have your freshwater tank, but how do you fill it, and how does it make its way through your camper? If you are hooked up to water at a campsite with a hose, that water will pressurize your system. If you are dry camping, you will have an onboard water pump that pressurizes the system. From here, water pipes provide a path to your faucets.

Let's touch on the difference between copper and PEX plumbing, your two piping options. Copper has been commonly utilized throughout plumbing systems because it is light, pliable, and relatively durable. But there are a lot of downfalls associated with copper piping, which ultimately led to the adoption of cross-linked polyethylene, or PEX. First, copper is a very expensive metal. If you were changing your copper piping to PEX piping throughout your house, you could turn the copper into a salvage yard and make a few hundred dollars. Also, installing copper piping requires a lot of skill and patience. Installers solder pieces together in supply runs.

Back in 1968, Thomas Engel invented PEX tubing. This noncorrosive plastic is preferred over copper plumbing for several reasons. We mentioned how expensive copper is compared to PEX. Well, using PEX will also save you a lot of money on your installation. Additionally, PEX is far more versatile than copper. PEX flexes and bends, allowing it to be installed in difficult locations. More so, its flexibility is an excellent feature for travel trailers, which can find themselves in freezing temperatures. The water can freeze, and because the tubing can easily expand and contract, there is less of a chance that it ruptures. Finally, PEX also has several adapters, allowing it to connect to preexisting copper, galvanized pipe, or PVC pipe, making modifications simple.

There are two types of PEX tubing: PEX A and PEX B. Type B utilizes a crimping tool to squeeze metal rings around a connection point (although new types of PEX B can be run with expansion connections). This ring prevents water from leaking. If you do not have a crimping tool, SharkBite push fittings can be used. This makes for quick installation. Simply push the pieces together. I would recommend the crimp tool route because it is more reliable and can stand up to higher pressures. Type A utilizes a specialized PEX expansion tool to stretch the tubing, allowing the installer to place the tubing on an elbow or appliance. Then, the PEX contracts tightly at the connection point, creating a leakproof seal. Because PEX A allows for more expansion, it is even more resistant to burst pressure, making it an even better choice in cold climates (and why I used it in this project). When selecting your elbows and T joints to route your PEX throughout your space, pay attention to which type of

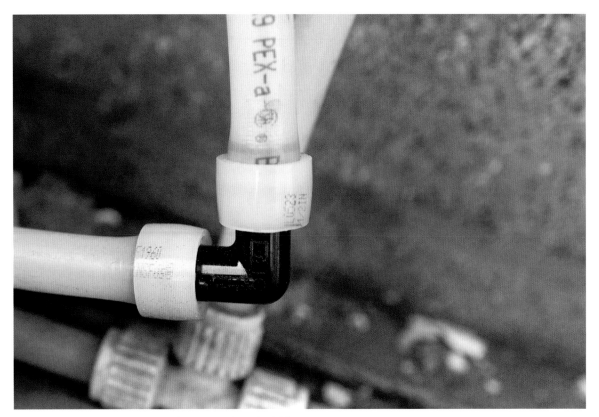

This is an example of what PEX tubing water lines look like.

PEX they are designed for. Please refer to the photos for installation details.

We spoke about filling your freshwater tank and utilizing PEX to plumb your system, but where does the water and waste go from there? New campers have both a gray tank and black tank. A gray tank is where your used water goes that is not considered sewage. The water and waste from the toilet will go to a black tank. This storage tank will have a valve that opens and closes and will allow you to hook a sewage hose to it and connect it to a waste station. Not all campers have black tanks and only utilize a gray tank, especially older models. Take our van as an example. Our gray tank was the same size as our water tank. All our gray water emptied into here. We used a cassette toilet for our sewage. This small portable toilet allows you to remove the cassette and empty it at a dump station or even a public toilet.

HOW TO INSTALL A CAMPER FRESHWATER SYSTEM

Materials and Tools

▷ **White freshwater tank with fittings and hoses**
▷ **½" (1.3 cm) PEX piping (Type A)**
▷ **PEX adaptors and fittings (match the piping size)**
▷ **Teflon thread sealing tape**
▷ **PEX expansion fitting tools**
▷ **New inlet valve**
▷ **Water fill**
▷ **Faucets and showerhead**
▷ **Tape measure**
▷ **Power drill and bits**
▷ **Crescent wrench**
▷ **Silicone sealant (optional)**

Instructions

1. Measure the space for your freshwater tank. Purchase the largest size tank that the space will accommodate. It is easiest to buy a tank complete with fittings and connections installed and hoses and hardware supplied. Secure your tank to the floor of the camper (making sure the wood is stable and rot-free) with the supplied brackets and nylon hold-down straps, following the manufacturer's instructions.

2. Modern campers and RVs usually have two sides to the plumbing system: the freshwater tank that is filled through an inlet port on the side of the body and a smaller fitting for city water that you connect to when docked, bypassing your freshwater system. Older camper trailers like mine do not usually have the

pressurized side, so you must combine the two. Rather than use the supplied 1⅜-inch (3.5 cm) inlet hose, I run a PEX line. To do that, you may need to replace the existing inlet port with one equipped with a one-way valve that will maintain pressurization. Unscrew the old one and clean the siding off thoroughly. Screw the new inlet port in place snug enough so that the base gasket creates a watertight seal (if it will not securely seal against the siding of your trailer, lay a bead of silicone sealant underneath it before tightening it down).

3. Run the PEX line from the inlet port to the water pump. Cut in a pipe tee fitting and run PEX to the tank fill inlet port. You will have to use a step-up fitting because the inlet ports on these tanks are meant to fit a 1⅜-inch (3.5 cm) hose.

4. Cut the PEX section between the pipe tee and the inlet port and splice it into a brass valve. To pressurize the system, I just close the valve. Open it for easy filling.

5. The freshwater tank has an outlet near the bottom. Run a PEX line from this outlet to the second inlet of the water pump (opposite where the pipe tee line runs into the pump). Make sure the water pump is securely screwed to the floor.

6. Finally, connect PEX to the opposite side of the brass valve pipe tee to route water throughout your camper's system.

7. Run PEX throughout the system, using clamps where necessary to hold the pipe in place (but always leave it loose enough to account for expansion and contraction). Spile in elbows, pipe tees, and straight-line couplings as necessary to extend lines or change direction. You will connect to your water heater, kitchen and bathroom faucets, toilet, and shower. I used expansion

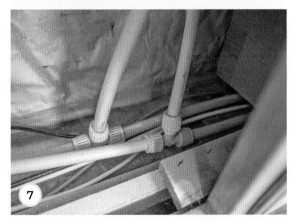

fittings and PEX B throughout, but you can use whatever type you prefer (crimp fittings can be a little hard to master). You can use push-fit fittings with either type of PEX. Regardless, use the same type of PEX throughout the entire system.

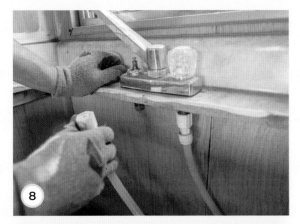

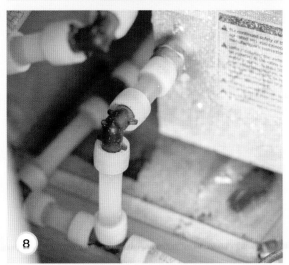

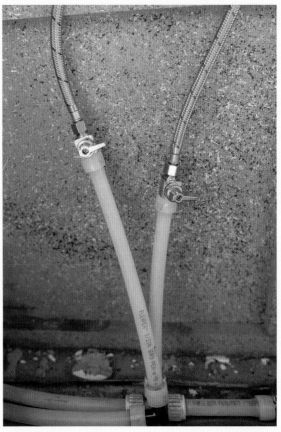

Petcocks are installed on the cold and hot water lines, allowing the system to stay pressurized while modifying a faucet, water heater, and so on.

PRESSURIZING THE SYSTEM

When you are sure that all connections are tight, pressurize the system by connecting a hose to your inlet. Check each connection, looking for leaks.

8. Some fixtures will have connections in varied sizes from the ½-inch (1.3 cm) PEX. In these cases, use step-up or step-down adapters available wherever you buy your PEX. Use Teflon tape on toilet, faucet, and shower connections to prevent leaks.

Propane

Propane is one of your primary energy sources. To be truly off the grid, you would not use propane because you do need to occasionally refill your tanks, but not very often. A standard 20-gallon (75.7 L) tank that you see in front of campers will last a while, especially if you are conserving. In the electrical section, I discussed how you can use electrical for your water heater, cooktop, and heater, but Chad and I have utilized both sources for each and prefer propane for a few reasons. Each tank will cost you $50 to $80 USD initially, but only $20 to $25 USD to refill. So, your initial setup will cost a lot less, something we are always a fan of.

Another reason is that propane goes a long way. If you are just cooking food and have a tankless water heater installed, your tanks will last for weeks. We usually carry three of these tanks: two for appliances and one for outdoor heating and cooking. If you are like us, cooking outdoors over a flame is one of our favorite parts of the camping experience. There is something freeing and primal about this, allowing you to let go of all life's stresses.

Lastly, refilling your tanks can be done just about anywhere. You will find propane refill stations in most towns, gas stations, and even campgrounds. It is important to know that these propane tanks have an expiration date, which is labeled on the head of the tank. We always exchange our tanks rather than refill them, so this is not an issue because the store keeps track the expiration date. If you plan to keep your tank and refill it, keep track of your expiration date.

Now that you know a little about the pros and cons of propane, let's talk a little about how the gas moves through your trailer. Your propane tanks will store this gas. From your tank, you will have a gas line running to a regulator. This regulator controls the amount of gas that can escape the tank. One nice feature to have is a fill meter, which will let you know how much gas is in each tank. These can be found on your line directly connected to your tank or on your regulator. This feature takes the guesswork out of your refilling needs. Chad is obsessed about things like this, always keeping our gas tank and propane on the full side.

From here, a flexible gas line will find a black iron line that will run into the trailer, just under the subfloor. If this black iron line, even though installed decades ago, is in decent shape still, that is one less thing for you to worry about. This black iron will intersect at several locations in your camper. From here, you will attach your copper or flex lines, which will run to the fridge, water heater, cooktop, and furnace.

When working with a flammable gas, safety is your top priority. Always make sure your propane tanks are off when modifying any lines or when the camper is not in use. At each threaded seam, make sure you use a thread sealant. This can be in the form of tape or putty. Chad prefers the putty (RectorSeal No. 5) because it is easier to apply and creates a highly effective seal.

Finally, ensure a tight connection at each fitting. Once the job is complete, turn on your propane tanks. At this point, make sure you do not smell gas in the air. Propane in the air is very easy to identify. Additionally, a viscous solution can be applied to the fittings where you will then look for bubbles. If bubbles are seen forming, you have a leak. It is always better to err on the side of caution with propane. If you suspect a leak, thoroughly investigate it!

Some fridges made for campers utilize propane to cool your fridge. This seems a little backward, right? The propane fridge operates on ammonia for the cooling cycle, and

◂◂ Built-in glass cover over propane stove

Using a propane stove in an RV

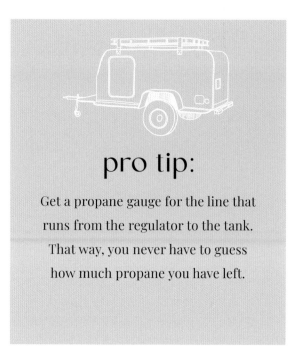

pro tip:

Get a propane gauge for the line that runs from the regulator to the tank. That way, you never have to guess how much propane you have left.

propane is used as a heat source to vaporize it. This method does take a little longer to cool the fridge initially, but once cooled, it is highly effective and efficient. Because the initial cooling takes some time, we put frozen meat we intend to cook that night in the fridge when we embark on our trip. As I mentioned in the electrical section, we prefer using a 12-volt fridge because they are cheaper and are very

efficient, and if you plan your solar setup correctly, you will have endless energy.

Propane cooktops and ovens are a great option for cooking. Depending on what you are cooking, one 20-gallon (75.7 L) propane tank will make weeks of freshly cooked meals. Chad loves cooking over a flame, so we always use a propane cooktop. We use the indoor cooktop for heating water for our French press or for making the kids some ramen as a nighttime snack. Actually, because we like cooking our meals outdoors so much, we actually remove the oven during our demo stage of a renovation and do not replace it. These ovens take up so much space and are heavy. A lighter camper is always a good idea.

Although we have used electric water heaters in the past, we've found that we prefer a tankless propane water heater. These things are so cool! The water heater only turns on when needed, heating the water on the spot. This eliminates the need for a pilot light and uses a lot less propane. When camping with hookups, you will have the luxury of endless hot water. This means you can take your time

Flame from a propane stove

when showering. If you are like me, a nice shower after playing in the dirt all day is very relaxing and makes long trips much more enjoyable.

On the other hand, when you are dry camping, a tankless water heater is less ideal than a tank water heater. Our 16-foot (4.9 m) trailer has a 21-gallon (79.5 L) freshwater tank, and this goes fast. Even though the tankless heats your water fast, you will still have it on for a few seconds. This is when a low-flow showerhead comes in handy, yet it still goes through water fast. A 0.5 gallon/minute (1.9 L/minute) showerhead will go through these 21 gallons (79.5 L) in forty minutes!

With both of us and the two boys, if we want to shower every day, we will need to refill our freshwater tank often. In our 16-foot (4.9 m) trailer, we opted to use a bidet head as a showerhead. This little guy saves a lot of water and is

only activated when you hold the trigger. The downfall of this is that it shuts the water heater off every time you release the handle, so you will be taking a cold shower. Obviously, that's not ideal.

With that said, if you want to conserve water, a 20-gallon (75.6 L) tanked water heater will make more sense—that way, you have hot water on hand when you are ready to shower. All four of us can take a quick shower with just 5 gallons (18.9 L) of water. You just need to get yourself wet; then turn the head off; then wash up with the water off; and then turn the water back on to rinse off quickly. This might seem less than ideal, but when you are off the grid, conservation is essential, and it is extremely rewarding knowing that you can live with so little.

Outdoor cooking is where it's at, and with propane, you have several options. We have a few outdoor cooking elements. Several brands make cast-iron cooktops that are heated with propane. This is a wonderful way to grill breakfast or, our favorite, make tacos! Open-flame grills are also an option, and some brands have both a grill and open flame available in one.

Finally, several fun outdoor heaters utilize propane. You can have an open-flame campfire to make s'mores and not have to deal with the smoke from a traditional campfire. They also make radiant propane heaters to make those cold nights more bearable.

Propane is flammable though. Always make sure your lines are free of propane when working on them and that your tanks are closed when working on your system. In short, you are running propane lines from your storage tanks to your appliances. It's that simple.

HOW TO INSTALL A PROPANE SYSTEM

Materials and Tools

- ▷ Two 20-gallon (75.7 L) propane tanks
- ▷ Propane regulator
- ▷ Propane hose adaptor
- ▷ Propane flex lines
- ▷ Copper or black iron propane line
- ▷ Interior propane flex line
- ▷ Pipe thread sealant (to seal threads, not flares) or Teflon thread sealing tape specified for LP applications
- ▷ Copper pipe tee adapters
- ▷ Crescent wrenches
- ▷ Gas leak detection spray or dish soap

Instructions

1. Secure the two propane tanks in the bracket on the tow hitch tongue. If your regulator has a single tank inlet, attach exterior flex lines to either side of a copper pipe tee fitting, using pipe sealant on the threads. Install a third flex line between the leg of the copper pipe tee and the regulator.

2. Attach the regulator to the bracket and connect an exterior flex line between the regulator outlet and the trailer's gas inlet.

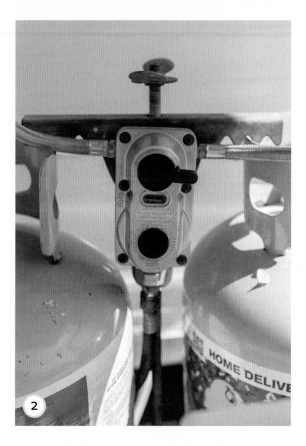

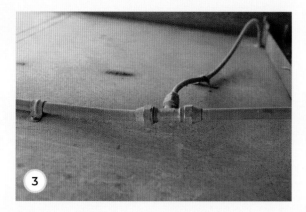

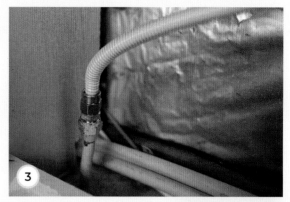

3. The interior main gas line will either be copper or black iron (copper is superior). It will run from the front of the trailer, under the floor, and divide into branch lines. The main line will have multiple outlets. (Unused outlets will be capped.) To connect an appliance, run a flex line from an uncapped outlet on the gas main to the appliance inlet.

4. If you smell propane when the gas is on, spray the connections with gas leak detecting spray or coat them with dish soap. If you find a leaking connection, disassemble it, clean the male and female threads, and reassemble with thread sealant or Teflon tape, tighten, and check the connection for leaks again.

Water Damage

When Chad and I came across the very first trailer we would renovate, we had absolutely no idea how to deal with water damage. Our only concern was that it was going to be cute, not thinking about what it meant to truly restore one of these classics. Little did we know that we were going to open the door to several learning opportunities—some simple, some challenging. Of those learning opportunities, water damage was a big one. The telltale sign is to look for discoloration or rippling in the panels.

Don't be afraid to push on areas you might be concerned about to see if they are soft. As scary as it may be to cut a hole in a perfectly good-looking panel, if you are suspicious at all of a water leak, do it! The last thing you want is to make your camper pretty and have to tear it up because of something you didn't want to deal with. Trailers are simple, and it is just a hole. You can and will be able to repair and patch it after finding and fixing any problem areas. You will need a few tools for this job, but most of them you probably already have.

Classic campers built with wood and metal components are susceptible to water damage due to their age and exposure to the elements. These trailers are not built like houses, and as they sit around for decades, the seams are bound to leak. Recently, our actual house had a roof leak. House roofs are rated for 10 to 30 years, and the amount of material that goes into preventing leaks on a house's roof is far more extensive than that on a travel trailer. These campers just don't stand a chance. But fear not: The same simplicity that makes them susceptible to leaks also makes repairs simple and generally low cost.

Obviously, the intrusion of moisture is found through compromised seals, seams, or vulnerabilities in the exterior shell. These can result from cracked or weathered caulk, damaged window seals, or rusted fasteners. Once water gains entry, it can wreak havoc on various components within the trailer. Now that Chad and I have done a few trailer renovations, we know all the hot spots. When I'm looking for the leak, I am always drawn to horizontal seams where water can puddle and to the bottom corners of the windows.

INTERIOR

The first noticeable signs of water damage often show up on the interior. The trailer's wooden substructure, including the floor and wall panels, is particularly vulnerable. Water can cause these materials to warp, rot, or delaminate, leading to structural instability and a potential safety hazard. Spongy or soft spots on the floor are a common indicator of water-damaged subflooring, making walking inside the trailer uncomfortable and unsafe. When you see water damage, it's pretty obvious. Just like most DIYers, it's easy to say, "It's not that bad, maybe I'll just paint over it!" Trust me, the small amount of time fixing any of these issues will be an investment that pays dividends for decades.

If you allow water to continue to penetrate the interior, it can impact the trailer's cabinetry and furnishings. Wooden cabinets may swell, warp, or develop mold and mildew. Upholstery and cushions can become waterlogged and musty smelling, requiring expensive restoration or replacement. Water stains on walls and ceilings can mar the trailer's appearance and reduce its resale value. Nine times out of ten, I look at Chad and say, "We are gonna rip it out!"

» This is a telltale sign of water damage in an RV.

Water also can lead to hidden issues as well. Insulation within the walls and ceiling may become saturated, losing its effectiveness and promoting the growth of mold, which we all know can be horrible for your health and challenging to remove completely. Removing mold can require a professional remediation service. No one likes mold, and if you see it, get your PPE on and just get rid of it.

In short, you will need to remove and replace damaged materials, reseal exterior seams and windows, and ensure the trailer is properly dried to prevent future issues. This can seem daunting, but with a little education and elbow grease, these repairs are not only doable, but they won't break the bank. Truth be told, the whole water damage process is a labor of love, but also very rewarding! I find that when I rebuild the walls, reframe the windows, and change every single screw on the rig, that I have given it a second life. You're not just slapping lipstick on a pig. You are doing the restoration right and creating something to be proud of, and you will walk away really knowing the ins and outs of the trailer.

EXTERIOR

To prevent water damage, regular maintenance of the exterior is essential. With vintage RVs, the siding is usually aluminum panels that are stapled into the 2 × 2 (5.1 × 5.1 cm) framing. As an owner of a classic travel trailer, you should inspect and reseal exterior seams, windows, and roof joints regularly and store it in a dry, protected environment when not in use. By taking proactive measures, you and your family can extend the life and beauty of these vintage treasures and utilize them to create memories to last a lifetime.

This process starts the same for every camper or RV. Inspect every seam where the exterior aluminum comes together. Unless you hit the gold mine, odds are you will have an incredibly old seal that should be replaced. Then, you will need new fasteners, butyl tape, silicone, and caulk. Let's take a step-by-step approach to do repairs and create a weatherproof shell.

Let's first talk about the long seams that span from the front of the camper to the rear. These connect the roofing to the siding. The two aluminum pieces come together at this seam, and a long aluminum trim piece is secured to not only hold the shell together, but to also create a waterproof seal. Depending on the length of your camper, you will need to remove and replace hundreds of screws. The monotony can be rough, so just put some music on and take joy in the idea that you are creating something great. So how do you remove the old, weathered fasteners and butyl that hold this trim in place? Here is how to effectively create a new long-lasting seal.

⇥ "Rippling" along the walls or ceiling is indicative of water damage.

HOW TO FIND, REPAIR, AND PREVENT WATER DAMAGE

Materials and Tools

- ▷ Driver and driver bits
- ▷ Power drill and bits
- ▷ Kreg pocket-hole jig
- ▷ Oscillating multitool
- ▷ Tape measure
- ▷ Stainless steel or zinc-coated screws
- ▷ Butyl tape
- ▷ Self-leveling lap sealant
- ▷ Exterior advanced paintable silicone caulk
- ▷ Plywood utility panel
- ▷ Waterproofing membrane (I like RedGuard and Tank/10.)
- ▷ Caulk gun
- ▷ Crown stapler and 1½" (3.8 cm) staples
- ▷ Scraper
- ▷ Wire brush
- ▷ Degreaser
- ▷ Dust mask
- ▷ Safety eyewear
- ▷ Work gloves

Exterior Instructions

RESEAL EXTERIOR SEAMS

1. Unscrew the existing trim with a driver and the appropriate bit. (I've used a ¼-inch [6 mm] hex bit for all my trailers.) Carefully pull back the aluminum trim by separating it from the original butyl tape.

2. Scrape the butyl tape off the trim piece and seam with a paint scraper and wire brush. Scrape and clean the seam on the trailer with a degreaser to remove any grease or dirt that may prevent the new butyl from adhering to the trim and trailer. (Any over-the-counter product will work; I use Krud Kutter or Simple Green.)

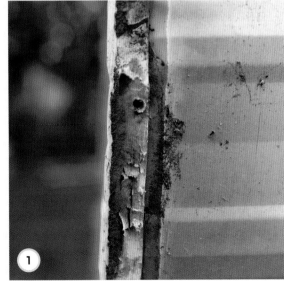

3. Apply new butyl tape to the back of the cleaned trim piece and reattach the trim.

Note: Butyl tape will line every section of any removable part on the exterior of the camper. That includes window frames, roof vents, the water heater door, fridge panels, and trim pieces, among other areas. The tape acts as a glue, sealing the exterior element to the camper. The new screws are driven through the tape, sealing the frame to the shell of the camper.

4. Secure the trim piece with new screws (I used 1 to 1½-inch [2.5 to 3.8 cm] #9 screws. If they don't securely hold, you may need to use larger ones such as 1 to 1½-inch [2.5 to 3.8 cm] #12 hex screws.) I use roofing screws because they have a weatherproof coating and small rubber washer. Stainless steel or wood screws will work as well. Don't use uncoated screws because they will rust over time. Select a screw size that is the same size as the original or just a bit bigger. This will allow the new screw threads to grab the aluminum siding and interior wood studs.

5. Once the trim is secured, apply a bead of exterior, paintable silicone to the top of the trim, where water could potentially puddle. Apply to both sides of the long frame side trim pieces.

RESEAL WINDOWS

1. To reseal windows, unscrew the frame and carefully pry the frame away from the trailer body. Inspect the studs to which the window is attached. If a stud is water damaged or compromised, use an oscillating multitool to cut out the rotted areas. Measure and cut a new 2 × 2 (5.1 × 5.1 cm) piece to replace the section you removed. There are two methods to fasten the new section into the existing stud. The first method is by toenailing. This simply involves nailing or screwing at a 45-degree angle, attaching new to the old. This is easy enough, but I would not recommend it. The 2 × 2 (5.1 × 5.1 cm) studs are lightweight wood and can split easily. The second method is by creating a pocket hole. A pocket hole jig is a handy tool used to create a clean diagonal screw hole. This creates a strong connection and prevents the stud from splitting.

4

2. Remove the old butyl tape from the trailer's exterior and from the window frame. Butyl tape is similar to putty and very sticky, which is why it is so good at preventing water intrusion. But that also makes it quite annoying to remove. Scrape it off and then run a stiff wire brush along the metal to remove any residual butyl tape and dirt.

3. Clean the window and frame with water and soap. Doing this with the windows removed allows you to get them much cleaner. I use a high-pressure hose nozzle to get into all the nooks and crannies. Clean the window frames exterior with degreaser.

4. Line the inside of the window frame with butyl tape. This is better than lining the opening because it allows you to most accurately place the butyl to ensure it passes directly over the screw holes. Replace the window with the weep holes on the bottom. This positioning is important because the holes allow water to flow away from the window. Screw the windows in place with new fasteners, ensuring the screws grab the trailer's frame securely.

4

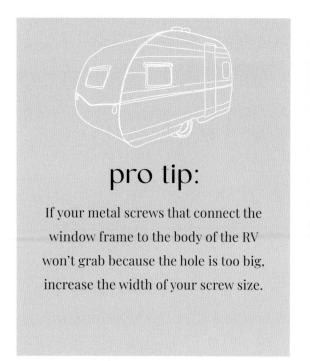

pro tip:

If your metal screws that connect the window frame to the body of the RV won't grab because the hole is too big, increase the width of your screw size.

5. Lay a bead of exterior, paintable silicone caulk on the seam between the window frame and trailer siding.

   Note: Around roof openings such as a vent, skylight, or roof-mounted AC, line the seams with a bead of self-leveling lap sealant. Several brands make this product. This sealant will be applied to the seams and over the screw heads after the units are installed. This is a weatherproof sealant that prevents water leaks. Once applied, it slowly spreads out a couple inches (5 cm), effectively sealing the seam. Because your roof is horizontal, it will likely have water puddling up on occasion. This self-leveling sealant might be the most important step in preventing future water intrusion from above.

Interior Instructions

REMOVING AND REPLACING DAMAGED STUDS AND WALLS

The section above assumes that the 2 × 2 (5.1 × 5.1 cm) framing does not have water damage. But what if it does? From the outside, it will be hard to tell if there has been water intrusion from an old, weathered seam. However, you definitely can find evidence of water damage in the interior. Inspect the interior walls around the windows or door panels, specifically at the corners. If water damage is present, you will commonly see discoloration, splintering, or warping of the utility panel walls. When the window is removed, you may find that the 2 × 2 (5.1 × 5.1 cm) stud is wet, soft, and rotting. Removing the old studs and replacing them with new is actually quite simple and absolutely necessary for the integrity of your trailer's frame. You can find inexpensive 2 × 2s (5.1 × 5.1 cm) and replacement plywood utility panel or MDF (medium-density fiberboard) for the walls at your local hardware store or lumberyard.

1. Use a Sharpie to mark where the rotted portion of the stud ends and the salvageable wood begins. Always overestimate where the rot ends. Removing an extra inch (2.5 cm) will not create any extra work and will ensure the screw holds securely. Do the same with the utility panel, attaching to the vertically running stud. You can locate studs by looking for the existing seams on the utility panel. These seams are usually covered with a small trim piece that is easily pried off. Be careful when removing the trim piece; you will likely reuse it to cover the seams after you put the new wall board up.

2. Wearing a dust mask, safety eyewear, and heavy-duty work gloves, use an oscillating multitool with a Japanese tooth blade and

cut out the damaged sections of the utility panel wall surface. Always make sure your trailer is not connected to power and be extremely careful to avoid cutting wires behind the walls. Set the multitool blade to the utility panel depth (⅛ inch [3 mm]).

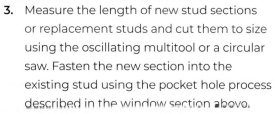

3. Measure the length of new stud sections or replacement studs and cut them to size using the oscillating multitool or a circular saw. Fasten the new section into the existing stud using the pocket hole process described in the window section above.

4. Once the studs are secure, it is time to rebuild your interior wall. The interior wall surfaces in these retro travel trailers are made of plywood utility panel. This is a very lightweight and flexible ⅛-inch (3 mm) plywood (lightweight being the key word here). This utility board can be found at your local hardware store. Attach the new panel to the exposed stud. A crown stapler with 1½-inch (3.8 cm) staples will make quick work of the job. To cover the seam, simply attach the old trim piece or new trim if you prefer.

Note: When removing old framing or wall panels, pay special attention to the possibility of black mold. This is crucial to the health of the occupants and the preservation of the trailer's structural integrity, so it should be treated the same as if you found it in your home. I think that most people see mold and their stomachs drop. Rightfully so. But in a trailer, you just need to put on the proper protective safety gear (including an approved respirator), cut out the compromised areas, replace with new material, and stop the leak that caused it in the first place.

REPLACING DAMAGED SUBFLOOR

1. Pull up any flooring over the damaged subfloor. Cut out the damaged section so that the patch will rest on a frame beam. (This may require removing more than the damaged section.)

2. Measure and cut the patch from the 4 × 8 (10.2 × 20.3 cm) sheet of plywood. Use a drill with a metal bit that matches the size of the other subfloor bolts to drill a hole or holes in the frame where you will secure the patch. Drill a matching hole in the patch. Bolt the patch in place and replace the flooring, if any.

Another excellent product for camper restoration is a waterproof membrane. This is a gel-like substance painted on wood that, you guessed it, waterproofs the wood. This membrane can be placed on the subfloor and walls where there might be a chance of water intrusion. I recommend painting a waterproof membrane on the subfloors in the bathroom and the wall of the showers. Another suitable place for this product is in your freshwater compartment or even the kitchen subfloor. Over time, small amounts of water consistently making its way through cracks in your bathroom floor will lead to rot and promote mold growth. The simple process of adding this membrane will protect your subfloor and allow for the water to evaporate. I have used both RedGard and Tank/10 with equal success. These are applied by just rolling it on like paint.

Waterproofing is a lot of work, but take pride in the work you put into this. When Chad and I are knee deep in the process, we just talk about previous camping adventures we went on and the ones to come. As a parent, you want to give your children as many core memories as possible. Camping with your kids is one of the surest ways to show them how to adventure and to give them those lasting memories they will think back on when they have a family of their own. That perspective always keeps us motivated, so find what yours is and remind yourself of them during the "not so fun" parts of renovating.

finding your style

Depending on whether you are drawn to the timeless elegance of traditional design, the sleek lines of modern aesthetics, or the bohemian charm of eclectic spaces, finding your design style is the first step toward making your tiny home a true expression of yourself. It is an exploration of colors, textures, patterns, and decor that align with your vision and create an environment where you feel truly at home.

But let's take a step back. What is your style? Do not be intimated! Discovering your design style is an exciting part of the RV renovation process that involves exploring your personal tastes, preferences, and the elements that resonate with you on an aesthetic level. Your design style should reflect your unique personality and lifestyle, and it plays a crucial role in creating spaces that are beautiful, comfortable, and functional. Different design styles can create entirely different moods in your space. So, make sure to pick designs that will be cohesive with the experience you hope to create and have.

In this section, I am going to run through what makes each design style unique in and of itself and the feeling that each evokes. There are entire books devoted to design, so my aim is not to cover it all. Rather, I will go over characteristics found in the most used interior design styles listed below in the hopes that it helps you identify what speaks to you. If I can save you some returns by homing in on your preferences ahead of ordering materials, that's the goal!

MID-CENTURY MODERN

Sometimes when I think of modern design, I think of a cold, echoing museum where you are not supposed to touch anything. Modern design is very sophisticated and at times can feel very sterile. It has a sense of seriousness with everything appearing clean and tidy. It can make you feel like nothing is relaxed or informal. This may sound horrible, but I promise it has many beautiful aspects to it as well. It is simple, functional, and uncluttered. Imagine how you feel after cleaning your house, picking everything up and putting it in its place— modern homes have less "stuff," which allows you to have that feeling more often than not.

This aesthetic embraces a clean, spacious layout, forming a canvas of elegance and practicality. You will find modern designs to be dominated by a neutral color palette, with grays and whites frequently used, accentuated by bold blacks and monochromatic accents. Sleek, minimalistic furniture emphasizing comfort and form takes precedence over function. The use of a slat wood wall, minimal to no hardware on cabinets, and unique lighting are ways to bring this into an RV or camper. Other materials such as glass, metal, and concrete can also contribute to a sleek, industrial look, while open spaces and abundant natural light create an inviting atmosphere.

This style is one that has grown on me with time, and when mixed with other design styles, I feel it can be part of a beautiful and inviting space. If you are one to enjoy a tidy and minimalistic lifestyle, this design style may be for you. If you are one to have a ton on your mind or feel overwhelmed easily, this may be a perfect design style to help you feel just the opposite. Having less knickknacks around may just help you become clearer minded in your everyday life!

BOHEMIAN

When I was about twelve years old, I wanted my bedroom to look like a bohemian princess lived there. I crafted a four-poster bed out of PVC pipe, draped some shear jewel-toned fabric on the corners, and hung a chandelier in the middle. I painted the wall a deep purple and had gold accents adorned with jewels. Wild, right? Well, boho interior design is just that: a captivating celebration of free-spirited creativity and an eclectic blend of global influences. It's all about throwing in lots of colors, patterns, and textures to make a space feel like a tapestry of adventures. Imagine rich, jewel-toned colors and fancy patterns on textiles and decor, plus layers of rugs, throws, and cushions for a comfortable vibe. Many of these things are easy to incorporate in an RV because they have more to do with decor than fixtures. Bohemian interiors are also big on indoor plants, bringing a touch of nature to your surroundings—again, something you can bring in after a renovation.

At the time of writing this book, the traditional boho decor has been toned down, and the most popular designs feature more neutral colors. Think decor that is heavy on jute rugs, raffia, rattan, pampas grass, and natural textures that weave nature into the design. Unlike some styles, boho design has few strict rules. Instead, it has a sense of freedom that encourages individuality and self-expression,

resulting in a space that says be yourself and get creative. People love how these spaces feel personal and cozy, giving almost a hippie vibe. It is commonly mixed with modern styles these days to create a unique blend that softens the characteristics of both. When this is done, it tones down the two very opposite extremes of each, into a cohesive modern boho look.

FARMHOUSE

If you have watched HGTV at any point in the last five years, you will be familiar with farmhouse style. It embodies a warm, earthy color palette, reminiscent of the countryside's natural beauty. Reclaimed wood and distressed finishes are used in the furniture and accents. I would say my favorite takeaways from this style are the rustic elements, such as barn doors and exposed beams frequently used that add character and history. (Yes, you can use both in an RV or camper!) The environment created in these spaces is cozy and functional, which promotes relaxation. I get a feeling of being home when walking in these spaces: You feel comfort and warmth. It is the perfect setting for creating cherished memories and embracing a simpler, more down-to-earth way of living. Okay, I admit I may feel that way because it is the style of my own parents' home, but bottom line, it often makes people feel like they are in a happy place.

You will undoubtedly find shiplap in these designscapes, usually painted white, accented with wood tones and black fixtures. This style catapulted to almost every household when home improvement shows made it famous, but the style features actually have been around for decades. The use of molding, chair rails, comfortable couches with chopped pillows, touches of greenery, window details, large basin sinks, and butcher-block countertops are a few other commonly used aesthetics that translate well to campers and RVs.

INDUSTRIAL

Many pubs, bars, and hip restaurants love this design style, probably because it creates a cool atmosphere. Industrial interior design is all about embracing a raw and unfinished look that highlights a building's structure: thin exposed brick walls, concrete floors, and visible ductwork. Unfortunately, many of those elements are not possible in an RV. But the ideas of those textures are a good guide to keep in mind if you love this style. Metal is a star player, with steel beams, pipes, and cool industrial light fixtures that add an edgy touch. (I have used faux brick paneling along with metal pipes and flanges to create brackets for shelving or light fixtures to re-create these features.)

The vibe is also open and spacious, often featuring lofty ceilings and large black framed windows. Again, this is tougher in a small space but possible to keep as a touchpoint for inspiration. Colors stick to the basics of grays, blacks, and browns, keeping things simple and highlighting natural materials. The furniture is functional and minimalistic, often in camel leather, incorporating industrial materials such as metal and reclaimed wood. Vintage or repurposed items add character, and statement light fixtures, such as exposed bulbs or cool pendants, play a significant role. The charm lies in celebrating the raw and unpolished aesthetic making for what many consider a traditionally "manly" environment. Whether you read it that way or not, there is no arguing that you see this design more for spaces without kids. It is a style that suggests a cool relaxed scene meant for adults.

MEDITERRANEAN

Mediterranean interior design evokes the sun-kissed coastal regions of southern Europe. Whenever I envision this style, I think of the iconic Santorini Islands with beautiful smooth architecture up against an ocean backdrop or a dream vacation at an upscale Caribbean resort. Throughout this book, you will see many examples of this design style as that was the theme of the RV I was renovating while writing. Mediterranean style creates a warm and inviting ambiance that captures the essence of leisure and relaxation. This design will transport you to a place of calm and serene surroundings. Commercially, it is commonly found throughout many winery tasting rooms and spa resorts. Rich, earthy color palettes that feature warm tones of terra-cotta, deep blues, and sea greens can be found on a natural-colored backdrop. Wrought iron, wooden furniture, and mosaic tiles contribute to the rustic charm, while arched doorways and textured walls add architectural character. The texture of the walls gives an old-world feel that is rough in texture but smooth throughout all the corners and curves. Abundant natural light and a strong connection to the outdoors bring a sense of open and airy living, promoting a relaxed and casual atmosphere. Mediterranean design will transport you to the idyllic landscapes of the Mediterranean, enveloping the space with a sense of timeless comfort and elegance.

With this design style, you can create a space that will make you feel relaxed and as if you were on a coastal vacation. It is sophisticated but comfortable at the same time. I love it because it can easily be weaved into many different styles and is timeless.

TRADITIONAL

I feel like this is a love it or hate it style. I admit it is usually not for me, although if done correctly, I can see the beauty in it. Traditional interior design is all about timeless charm and a warm, classic ambiance. It can give off a classic royalty vibe as if you were at Buckingham Palace. Picture ornate furniture with fancy details such as carvings and turned legs, often arranged in pairs for a balanced look. The color palette leans toward rich tones such as deep reds and blues, with touches of gold and classic neutrals, such as beige. You will find lots of patterns, from florals to stripes, especially on things such as curtains and rugs. Antique and vintage pieces are key to adding character and a touch of history. Rooms are usually set up with a formal and symmetrical layout, and there is a love for natural wood finishes. Elaborate molding and trim on walls and furniture add a classy touch, and traditional interiors often play with various textures for depth. Think grand chandeliers and elegant lighting fixtures, plus formal heavy drapes for the windows. It all comes together to create a comfortable, sophisticated, and timeless feel.

Traditional style can give a very upscale and beautiful look if done correctly, but it can also tend to look like "grandma's house" if you add too much frill or dated fabrics. Depending on your upbringing, it can give you a sense of comfort as if you are back home at your family's house. This design can give a great sense of nostalgia, but if you don't like intricate details or rich bold touches, this style is not for you.

COASTAL

Being a California girl, this style is comforting to me, bringing the beach into your home and creating a relaxed and breezy vibe. Imagine light and airy colors inspired by the sea, such as soft blues, greens, and sandy neutrals, creating a bright and open feel. Coastal interior design usually displays lighter wood tones, tons of windows, and French doors with sheer flowy curtains. Often the use of surfboards, boat oars, and lifeguard-tower inspired furniture will be seen. Natural materials, such as wood and rattan, add a beachy touch, often with weathered finishes for that laid-back look. Nautical elements, such as stripes and sea-themed accessories such as rope lighting, contribute to the coastal charm and are commonly used. Almost all this can be incorporated in a camper or RV.

Furniture is all about comfort in coastal style, with casual slipcovered sofas and wicker pieces. The fabrics are light and breezy, and you will often find sea-inspired decor, such as seashells and driftwood. Coastal spaces are open and inviting, with a focus on natural light and a casual, easygoing atmosphere. It is like a seaside getaway right in your own home, complete with the soothing sense of the ocean.

This is a great style for those wanting to live the epitome of a beach bum life—minus the beach. It creates a very family-friendly, comfortable, fun, and laid-back environment with nothing too structured.

SOUTHWESTERN

Southwestern interior design brings the warmth and colors of the American Southwest into your home by using earthy tones such as terra-cotta and deep blues to create a cozy atmosphere. Natural materials such as wood and stone give a rustic touch, and you will find vibrant textiles with bold geometric patterns inspired by Native American and Mexican influences. You can personalize it with handcrafted items, from pottery to textiles. Large windows bring in natural light, connecting your space to the wide landscapes of the region. Wrought iron accents, cacti, and kiva fireplaces contribute to the Southwestern charm. (I *love* the organic look of a kiva fireplace.) Aside from the large windows, almost all these elements are camper- and RV-friendly.

This style celebrates cultural influences by using artifacts and vivid patterns to create a welcoming and unique interior that reflects the richness of the Southwest's history and artistry. It is heavy in desertscapes using the rich colors of a sunset.

With this design style, you can create multiple feelings: It can be moody with the rich colors, livestock, and leather fabrics or very down to earth with smooth plaster walls and the use of pottery and wooden decor. It is a calming space that to me seems to be for someone comfortable in solitude. It is a soothing style that is rich in history.

Creating a Mood Board

A mood board is a visual way to gather and organize ideas, inspiration, and design elements for a project. This visual tool will help you clarify your design vision, gather inspiration, and make cohesive project choices so that the result will make you happy.

Start by defining the purpose of your space and the theme or interior design style you want to go with. Whenever I begin my mood board, I head straight to Pinterest and start looking up the style I am going for. For example, if I wanted to go with a coastal RV style, I would type that into the search bar and start a collection of different photos that resonate with me within that style. It could be a great color palette, a wallpaper used in a photo, captivating light fixtures that fit that theme, or even just hardware used on cabinets in the photos. Look for images related to your chosen style, capturing colors, textures, patterns, and overall vibes that align with your vision.

Once I collect a good number of images, I then look at them as a whole to find common features or patterns that I am being drawn to. You also can search many different online platforms, magazines, or places you see throughout your city (or even scenery) for inspiration.

Next, I highly recommend using an online platform to be able to see distinctive design elements come together in one space side by side. I currently use Canva, which is extremely easy to use and convenient for this purpose. From there, I narrow down options for each element of the design. This can include images of furniture, color swatches, fabric samples, light fixtures, rugs, flooring, and tile. Pay attention to the balance and composition of your selections to create a cohesive and visually appealing layout. So many times, I think something will go perfectly until I lay it all out together and realize something clashes. It is much better to have this happen in the planning stage rather than after you purchase things and have them ready to install, just to find out it will not work. When arranging the items, do so in a manner as if you were walking into the space, with lighting up top, flooring on the bottom, and the background canvas being the paint color. Consider the scale and proportion of the elements on your mood board, ensuring they reflect the intended balance and harmony of the actual space.

If doing all this online is out of your comfort zone, the same thing can be achieved by getting a poster board and cutting out unique features you see from a magazine. You can move them around and swap things out until it looks right. Also, I have found getting real tile samples, flooring pieces, fabric swatches, and actual cabinet hardware or light fixtures all laid out together is another way to dial in on a mood board.

These steps help convey the tactile and visual elements of your design. Feature key elements such as furniture pieces, lighting fixtures, or architectural details to provide a focused representation of the essential components contributing to the overall mood. Review your mood board, checking for coherence and ensuring that the elements work harmoniously together. Adjust as needed, refining the composition until it accurately represents your design vision. Once you get to a place where all the elements are on your board and it looks cohesive, you can start sourcing all the things needed to get your renovation done. This is always exciting and frustrating at the same time because it can be difficult to find exactly what you want at a reasonable price.

Note that having a certain light fixture on your mood board doesn't mean that you will end up with that exact one. When originally pulling inspiration, I never focus on price tags because at this point I'm just trying to nail down "the look." So many times, I am gathering inspiration and find something that is thousands of dollars. However, the point is to lock down the look you are going for and then to find something similar in style at a bargain. It is a fun game to see how closely I can get to the original inspiration at the lowest price.

Last, not only should the tangible decor be something you think about when creating a space, but I also never discount the smells you bring into the space. This is something most overlook, but including all your senses into a design will immerse you into it even more. Adding cucumber melon scents to a coastal design, lavender candles in a space you want to be relaxing, or a mahogany cedar candle in a manly space will just take your design to the next level.

If you do this step at the beginning of any project, big or small, I promise you will go into the renovation with a much stronger grasp on where you are heading, and the end results will be evident of that.

An example of a mood board to show a cohesive look

flooring and ceilings

So much of design is figuring out everything you want to include between your four walls. Two especially key areas that make or break your space are sometimes an afterthought: the ceilings and the floors. Look at this as the shoes and jewelry of your masterpiece! You can add so much character in these areas, whether it be by laying flooring in a unique pattern such as herringbone or by adding an eye-catching feature on the ceiling to draw your eye up. I will discuss my favorite flooring that I always use along with some super fun projects that can be done to your ceiling to really take things up a notch in your design.

Flooring

The flooring you choose will be what grounds your space and is a huge decision when choosing color tones and types. One of the main considerations is picking a material that is durable and resistant to big temperature changes that can come with traveling in an RV. Many RVs come with carpet laid throughout, which *does* give a warm and cozy feel but harbors the dirt and debris that is commonly tracked into these small spaces. I say, "No thank you!" Another option you may have seen is glue down flooring, which I would advise against doing in RVs as the drastic temperature changes and movement are bound to cause separation and a peeling up mess in the end. Vintage RVs that I have remodeled usually have linoleum laid throughout. Another common flooring seen in RVs nowadays is laminate or vinyl flooring, which is always what I install in my renovations.

Original floors before adding LVP

Original flooring before renovations

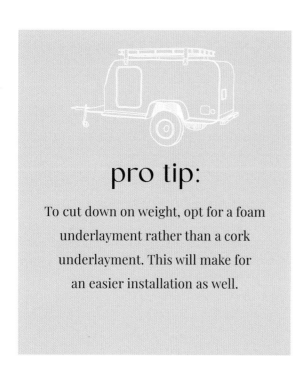

pro tip:

To cut down on weight, opt for a foam underlayment rather than a cork underlayment. This will make for an easier installation as well.

New LVP floors installed

New LVP floors installed

LUXURY VINYL PLANKING (LVP)

Many different types of flooring options are available, but I always stick to luxury vinyl planking when sourcing for my RV renovations. This option is perfect for RVs as it is a floating floor that will allow for swelling with temperature changes and movement in a trailer. LVP is made of vinyl, but the look and texture really mimic the look of real hardwood material. On top of that, it is incredibly durable, making for easy cleanups and limited maintenance. This makes for a perfect product when you want a homey vibe that wood floors bring along with the ability to easily clean and maintain your flooring. Another great perk is that you can find many options to fit your style and it is easy to install!

When making my selection, here are a few things I keep in mind:

1. **Color and texture:** I always prefer to go into a store to get my flooring. LVP can be smooth or have an actual texture that mimics wood grain. This makes it so much more realistic and adds character. Running your hands on the product is the only way to get a feel for it. Regarding the color, I try to find planks that have variation and multiple colors within the same tone. This really helps disguise dust and dirt that may be on the floor, so you do not feel like you have to constantly clean.

2. **Underlayment:** When picking out LVP, I always opt to get one that has the underlayment attached. This is the material that you put underneath the LVP to give padding, act as a sound-absorbing layer, and provide moisture resistance. If you buy it separately, it comes in a roll, and you lay it

out underneath where the flooring will go. Take it from me: Get the planks that have it attached to save yourself a headache.

3. **Installation type:** Your best bet is to choose a click-lock or floating LVP to use in RVs. Stray away from glue down and peel-and-stick LVP as it will separate. The floating floor has a small gap around the perimeter that is covered by shoe molding or a baseboard, which will allow for swelling, but the locking mechanism keeps the flooring together securely.

4. **Thickness:** Depending on your RV, you may need to be conscious of the thickness of the LVP you choose. In vintage RVs, this isn't too much of an issue, but if you are replacing the flooring in a newer RV that has slide-outs, you need to get a thinner LVP to ensure the slide mechanism will not scratch the LVP when pulled in. LVP comes in 2 mm to 8 mm (0.1 in to 0.3 in) thickness, and I usually get around 5 mm (0.2 in)-thick LVP.

5. **Tips and tricks:** Due to vintage RVs having an exceedingly small footprint, you can get lucky at local flooring stores that may have remnant products for a discounted price or even free at times. Always measure 10 percent over what you need to account for cuts. Having a multitool to make intricate cuts is also extremely helpful during installation.

VINYL SHEETING

Another option that is similar to what many vintage RVs originally have is vinyl sheeting. You can find many assorted designs printed on vinyl sheeting that mimic the look of wood flooring or tile. They are found at most big-box home improvement stores in huge rolls that are about 12 feet (3.7 m) wide. You buy the length needed for your RV, which will be the length of your RV. The difficult part is creating a template to cut the vinyl to the shape of your flooring in one piece. Many measurements at multiple points are needed, and a tip I have received is to cut it slightly larger at first. Then bring it inside the RV and trim off the excess as you need to get a precise fit. At that point, you will be ready to glue it down with the appropriate adhesive.

The benefits of this flooring is that it is lightweight, waterproof, and easy to clean and maintain. You will not see separation, as it is one piece, and vinyl sheeting has come a long way in the designs offered to look more realistic to wood flooring. This is also a very affordable option.

HOW TO LAY LUXURY VINYL PLANK FLOORING

Materials and Tools

▷ Luxury vinyl plank flooring (I like thin flooring, around 5 mm, [0.2 in] with underlayment attached.)
▷ Shoe molding
▷ Drill and drill bits
▷ Brad nails
▷ Wood putty
▷ Oscillating multitool
▷ Rubber mallet
▷ Pull bar
▷ Tapping block
▷ Spacers
▷ Contour gauge
▷ Tape measure
▷ Utility knife
▷ Ruler
▷ Dust mask
▷ Safety eyewear
▷ Work gloves

Instructions

1. Measure the square footage of the space by multiplying the length by the width. Normally, you should add 10 percent for waste, but for LVP, this measurement will suffice and will ensure you have the extra flooring needed to account for cuts.

2. Allow the boxes of flooring to acclimate in the camper for at least twenty-four hours. Decide which direction you want to lay your flooring. Lengthwise is usually a more appealing look and limits the number of cuts you will need to make.

3. Next, open all the flooring boxes and separate the different patterns. There are usually about five patterns; vinyl plank flooring is made with a printed design that repeats. You want to ensure that you do not use the same "print" of planks right next to each other. In the photo above, you can see their are no repeating patterns in the finished floors. I separate all the planks into different patterns and alternate pulling from each pile as I lay the flooring.

4. Lay the first row. This is a step all in its own because it is the most important row; it sets the tone for the rest of the rows. It needs to be straight. Start the first plank on the longest straight edge in the trailer. This is usually in front of the kitchen or bench seats in a vintage trailer. Use spacers between the flooring and cabinet edges; these will be removed once the flooring is laid. The gap you maintain allows the floating floor to move as it expands and contracts. Use shoe molding or baseboards to cover the gap.

5. The individual planks in the row simply click together end to end. You will click and lock in the planks in the next row, along the sides, and at the ends. Cut the first planks to stagger each row's pattern and so no seams align. Cut the starting boards about ⅓ the length of the previous starting plank. Lay in rows from the inside corner, working your way to the door-side wall. To fit planks in tight situations, use a rubber mallet and pull bar. This allows you to click in the edge pieces that are difficult to install.

6. To cut planks, clearly mark the surface with a pencil and a speed square. Score with a utility knife and snap to break the plank. Thicker planks may require a miter saw. Use painter's tape on the cut line to avoid tearing it out.

7. Pros use an undercut jam saw to make a space for the plank to slide under door casing. However, I chose to use a contour gauge to capture the profile of the casing and then cut a notch in the flooring to fit.

7

7

8. Allow the floor to sit for eight to twenty-four hours and then finish it with shoe molding. I used three-quarter round molding, which is the easiest option to conceal the expansion gap along the edge of the floor. Measure and cut the molding lengths with a miter saw, using a splice cut on the ends of any sections that will be mated. Drill pilot holes and nail the molding in place with brad nails to the wall, not the floor. Dab the nail heads with wood putty, sand smooth when dry, and paint or stain the molding as you prefer. You also can create baseboards with ¾-inch (19 mm) profile molding if you want a more upscale look, depending on whether you have enough clearance for a higher piece of molding.

8

Ceilings

So many times, people neglect the "fifth" wall in a space. I love to do creative accents in RVs to make them unique. I first landed on adding a design to a ceiling in my first RV renovation when I was forced to produce a solution to fix damage I created by ripping out cabinets. Vintage RVs are built from the inside out, so when you go to remove cabinets, you will notice screws and crown staples coming down from the ceiling, as if they were all secured before the aluminum shell was attached. This makes this hardware very difficult to remove because you can't remove the screws properly to remove cabinets. Even though this was such a headache trying to figure out how I would repair the nail holes, it forced me to get creative and design a molding layout to cover those spots. This was something I never would have done. There are many different options to use on ceilings, and I will go over a few I have tried with success.

FAUX BEAMS

Whether it is a house, RV, or shed, I would opt to have wood beams in every space. This is my favorite addition to any design, and the wonderful thing is that it can work with any design style you choose. You can keep them modern and sleek or distress them to fit more into a coastal or rustic design. Another great thing is you can customize them to your needs very easily. When planning out your beam, placement and size depends upon a few things. Do you have tall or standard ceiling height? Vintage RV ceilings are about 7 feet (2.1 m) tall, so you would only want to drop a beam down a couple inches (5 cm). Newer RVs can have quite tall ceilings, so you have more options on the depth of your beam. However, be conscious of weight when making this choice. I always make my beams with 1 × 2 (2.5 × 5.1 cm) sides attached to ¾-inch (19 mm) wood, which makes the beam drop 2¼ inches (5.7 cm).

Molding pattern added to an RV ceiling

Faux wood beams in a toy hauler RV

Faux beams in a vintage camper

The other decision you need to make is the width of your beam. I use pine to create the beams and usually use 1 × 6s (2.5 × 15.2 cm), giving me a 5½-inch (14 cm)-wide beam. Decide if you want a 1 × 4 (2.5 × 10.2 cm), 1 × 6 (2.5 × 15.2 cm), or 1 × 8 (2.5 × 20.3 cm) for the fronts of your beams. The last decision to be made is how many to add. If you look at the ceiling, you can see where the panels meet, every 4 feet (1.2 m). I usually cover those seams with a beam. The most important thing is to only place a beam where a cross stud runs, to which you can attach the beam supports. On pages 87–89, I will show you the steps I take to create my faux beams that will not add an extreme amount of weight to your RV but will add a ton of character. This is a great beginner tutorial, keeping it simple, but if you feel up for the challenge, you can choose to miter the long edges of your wood to give a seamless joint when assembled.

SHIPLAP

Shiplap is not just for walls! It is a super easy way to add a little something extra to your space. If you use shiplap vertically on the walls, it looks clean and cohesive to run the shiplap in the same line across the ceiling. This will draw the eye up and make your ceilings appear taller than they are. When securing shiplap to a ceiling, you will want to use an adhesive and brad nails or crown staples. Ripping your own shiplap down is also necessary as premade shiplap is far too heavy. I rip my own shiplap down from ⅛-inch (3 mm) utility board into 6-inch (15.2 cm) strips. You should be able to get about seven to eight strips that are 8 feet (2.4 m) long from one board.

Another option is to use the shiplap boards in a design rather than just laying them in a traditional shiplap pattern. You can mimic a coffered ceiling design with the shiplap pieces and even add in different molding pieces to give a more intricate design.

TIN OR BAMBOO

Tin and bamboo are two options for ceilings that I personally have never used, but they are great choices. Tin sheets can be found at most big-box home improvement stores. They are lightweight and simple to install, yet on the pricier side, which is the biggest downfall. These are a perfect addition to a traditional design style that would have intricate molding features. Also, they come in many gold and metallic shades that could be perfect for a moody dark space to add the perfect character.

Bamboo is another option to add to the ceiling. I have seen this done only in houses, but the lightweight features are perfect for an RV. You can use a bamboo garden fence, so the bamboo shoots are secured together and can be rolled out and secured to the ceiling. This would be an amazing accent to add in a coastal, Mediterranean, or boho design—especially if it is laid between faux beams to give an upscale tiki vibe!

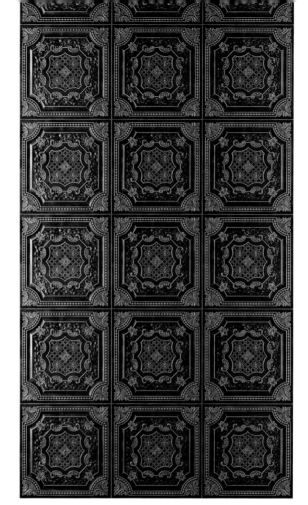

Tin sheets

Bamboo added to a ceiling

WOOD PLANKING

I stumbled across the perfect cedar planking at the Home Depot to use in RVs. It is lightweight and inexpensive, and it smells amazing! I have used it multiple times, and it is once again very customizable to many unique design styles, by staining a lighter or darker color. This is something I have used when having to rip out a ceiling due to water damage. Wood planking is also perfect to add to a ceiling in a smaller space, such as the bathroom. The planks are tongue and groove and interlink, so it is a solid surface when installed. Secured with crown staples, wood planking is a quite simple upgrade you can do to that underrated fifth wall in your space. I left these ones natural, but you can add a pop of color if you like.

Installing cedar planks on a ceiling

Finished cedar planks in RV bathroom

Cedar planks in van conversion

HOW TO BUILD AND INSTALL FAUX BEAMS

Materials and Tools

- ▷ (1) 8' × 1" × 4" (2.4 m × 2.5 cm × 10.2 cm) pine (for each beam front), or substitute 1" × 6" (2.5 × 15.2 cm) or 1" × 8" (2.5 × 20.3 cm)
- ▷ (2) 8' × 1" × 2" (2.4 m × 2.5 cm × 5.1 cm) pine board (for beam sides or substitute 1" × 3" (2.5 × 7.6 cm) 1" × 4" (2.5 × 10.2 cm) as desired
- ▷ (1) 8' × 2" × 4" (2.4 m × 5.1 cm × 10.2 cm) pine nailing
- ▷ Tape measure
- ▷ Pencil or sharpie
- ▷ Wood glue
- ▷ Bondo wood filler
- ▷ Power nailer
- ▷ Brad nails
- ▷ Clamps (the more you have, the easier)
- ▷ Wood stain
- ▷ Polyurethane
- ▷ Orbital sander
- ▷ 110- and 220-grit sanding discs
- ▷ 400-grit sanding block
- ▷ Impact driver
- ▷ Respirator or N95 dust mask
- ▷ Safety eyewear
- ▷ Work gloves

Instructions

1. Locate the studs or seams on the ceiling; this will determine how many beams you place. Measure the width of your trailer at each spot. These will be the lengths of each individual beam.

2. Determine how wide you want each beam. This project creates smaller beams using 1 × 4s (2.5 × 10.2 cm). Also determine how low you want the beams to hang. This may depend on the headspace you want or cabinet door swing. Here, I built shallow beams with 1 × 2 (2.5 × 5.1 cm) sides.

3. Use one 8-foot (2.4 m) pine board of the desired width, for each beam (1 × 4s [2.5 × 10.2 cm] here). Use two 8-foot (2.4 m) boards in the desired depth (1 × 2 [2.5 × 5.1 cm] here). Cut the three boards to the length of each beam.

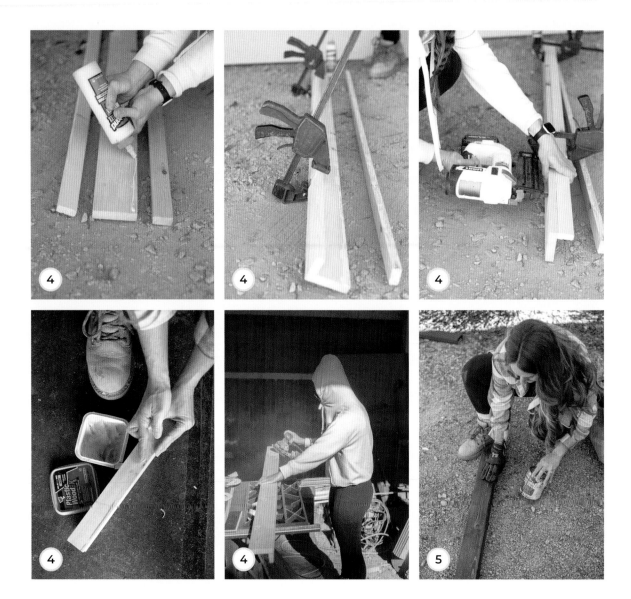

4. Run a bead of wood glue along the long edges of the wider board. Clamp the boards to form them into a *U* shape, with edges flush. Nail the joints with brad nails spaced every 6 to 8 inches (15.2 to 20.3 cm). Wipe away any excess glue and let dry overnight. Use Bondo wood filler to fill all nail holes.

Optional: Distress the beam with chains, hammers, wood chisels, and/or wire brushes. Use an orbital sander and 110-grit sandpaper to round the edges and even everything out. Follow up with 220-grit.

5. Stain in the shade you prefer if you are staining. Let the stain dry fully and apply two coats of clear poly, sanding lightly with a 400-grit sanding block between applications.

6. Measure the inside width of the beam and cut nailing cleats 6 inches (15.2 cm) long to fit inside. Screw to the studs or solid surface of the ceiling, being careful not to screw through the roof along the centerline of the beam. Mark cleat locations with painter's tape.

7. Slide the hollow beam over the cleats and nail in place with brad nails.

paint

———

Not every RV needs to be painted from top to bottom. However, if you do choose to tackle this project, it is one that can create the biggest changes for a fairly low amount of money! When you go to choose the paint for your space, keep in mind that it is what will set the tone for your design. Do you want an airy, light feeling upon walking in? Maybe you want more of a moody escape that is as cozy as if you were fireside in the forest! I usually recommend starting out with a more neutral color throughout: whites, beige, gray, or even black. You can always add pops of color by adding a bold accent wall or colorful decor. Having a cohesive base color throughout your RV will make the space flow together more seamlessly.

Painting RV Walls

Painting the interior walls of an RV can be a fantastic way to upgrade the look and feel of the space. For example, a quite simple way to make a small space appear to be larger is by painting a light color throughout. It will bring more light into the area and really gives you a blank, clean slate to work with.

Most campers come standard with wood paneling throughout, and so by doing this one project, it can really make a huge difference with minimal expense. Although this project won't break the bank, you should follow many steps to clinch those long-term goals of keeping this paint upgrade from chipping away.

RV walls typically have 4 × 8 (1.2 × 2.4 m) panels that are placed vertically with trim pieces between them. They are made from very thin wood or composite material in a lot of vintage RVs. Many use laminated panels that consist of a lightweight, rigid substrate, such as utility board, which is sandwiched between decorative layers. The decorative layers can be vinyl, wallpaper, or other materials that provide the desired aesthetic.

In every camper renovation I have done, I always start out by removing all the cabinet doors, drawers, and lighting. This allows me to demo what I need, make structural repairs, and then be ready to paint everything. I tend to go with a soft white so that it acts as a good base to build off, adding in color as I go per my design board.

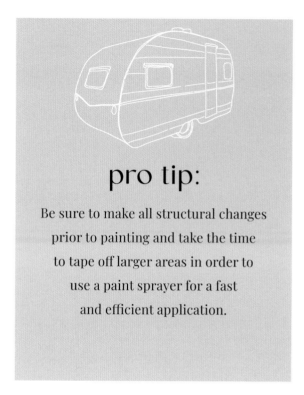

pro tip:

Be sure to make all structural changes prior to painting and take the time to tape off larger areas in order to use a paint sprayer for a fast and efficient application.

Using high-quality paint is key when painting RV walls. Use an eggshell or satin finish to ensure the surface is cleanable in these high traffic tiny homes on wheels. My recommendations for paints are in the tutorial on page 93.

So, what are the complete steps to getting that perfect paint job that will last over time? I will break down my process below showing you the steps to follow when embarking on painting your RV walls.

HOW TO PAINT RV INTERIOR WALLS

Materials and Tools

▷ **Water-based paint (I like Sherwin-Williams Duration or BEHR MARQUEE, which is a paint and primer in one, or ULTRA SCUFF DEFENSE.)**

▷ **Water-based primer (I like Zinsser 1-2-3 Water-Based Primer.)**

▷ **Water-based matte polyurethane (I use Varathane.)**

▷ **Paintbrushes and rollers, or a paint sprayer (I like Wagner FLEXiO Series sprayers.)**

▷ **Painter's tape**

▷ **Drop cloths or plastic sheeting**

▷ **220-grit and 600-grit sandpaper**

▷ **Bondo wood filler (as needed)**

▷ **High flexibility painter's caulk (such as DAP Extreme Stretch Sealant)**

▷ **Tack cloth**

▷ **Clean, lint-free cloth**

▷ **Surface cleaner (I use TSP [trisodium phosphate].)**

▷ **Screwdrivers**

▷ **Box wrenches**

▷ **Power drill and bits (optional)**

▷ **Dust mask**

▷ **Safety eyewear**

▷ **Work gloves and latex gloves**

Instructions

1. Remove hardware, fixtures, or anything else attached to the walls, including light switch plates, outlet covers, curtain rods, and decorations. If you're not demo'ing the entire interior, cover surfaces and furnishings with drop cloths or plastic sheeting. (I use painter's plastic that buy in 400-foot [121.9 m] rolls for about $25 USD; one roll has lasted through years of projects, so worth the small investment.)

2. Tape off windows with plastic and remove the frames. In older RVs, you can easily unscrew the metal frame. In newer RVs, tape the exterior to ensure it doesn't fall out when removing the interior window frame. Although modern water-based paints release very little fumes or odors, it's wise to wear appropriate safety gear, including a mask, safety eyewear, and gloves.

3. For a much more seamless look, run a bead of painter's caulk along all trim seams. This will ensure gaps will be less visible once painted. I like DAP Extreme Stretch Sealant because it is very flexible and will move with the trailer.

4

6. Tape off any areas you don't want painted, such as trim, windows, or adjacent walls. Be thorough and precise to ensure clean paint lines. This is especially important if you are using a paint sprayer.

7. Prime the surfaces to ensure bonding of the top coat. The primers I listed earlier help paint adhere better to RV walls, and they can prevent stains from bleeding through. Follow the manufacturer's instructions for the specific primer you choose. Apply a coat of primer with a ⅜-inch (10 mm) nap roller and angle paintbrush and allow it to dry per the manufacturer's instructions, typically twenty-four hours.

8. If painting by hand, start by cutting in around the edges of the walls with a brush. Paint corners, edges, and areas near the tape first. Then, use a foam roller to paint larger wall surfaces. Apply the paint evenly, working in small sections.

   Optional: If you are using a paint sprayer, start with the ceiling and work down. This is the quickest way to work, but also requires the most prep.

9. Apply a second coat if necessary for even coverage. Allow the paint to dry fully between coats, following the manufacturer's recommended drying times. I stay out of the camper for at least twenty-four hours after painting.

10. Carefully remove the painter's tape while the paint is still slightly wet. I remove the window plastic first to open the windows and provide ventilation. Inspect the walls for any imperfections or missed spots and touch up as needed.

4. Fill any nail holes or damage to the walls with wood filler. I use Bondo wood filler. It is a two-part mixture that is strong and dries fast but has a potent smell.

5. Clean the walls thoroughly to remove dirt, grease, and residue. I use a mixture of TSP and water diluted to the recommendations on the bottle and applied with a damp cloth.

   Scuff the walls lightly with 220-grit sandpaper to create a good surface for paint adhesion. Repeat the cleaning process with TSP to remove dust after sanding.

   Let it dry completely before painting.

Painting Camper Cabinets

Painting cabinets in an RV is very similar to painting the walls but with a few extra steps. I recommend an eggshell to satin finish on cabinets. This allows for easier cleaning than a matte finish would. You can, however, apply matte polyurethane for a less shiny finish that is still cleanable.

Most RV cabinets are a thin laminate material, so it is essential to prep and prime correctly. You want to avoid your hard work scratching off with the first pull at a handle. When prep sanding, make sure to go light enough to only scuff the surface. If you go too deep, you can damage the top layer veneer.

When picking your cabinet color, reference your mood board. Keep to the style that resonates with the overall look you are going for. Be mindful of the countertop color because a good contrast is always appealing. Two-toned cabinets are a great way to incorporate a darker color on the base cabinets and a lighter color on the uppers to keep the space feeling airier.

Different techniques can be done as well, such as a faux wood glaze, cane webbing inserts, or adding molding to modernize older cabinet doors. The prep process for these techniques is the same.

Let's dive into all the steps you should take to paint your cabinets in your camper.

Faux wood painted cabinets

Pale pink painted cabinets

HOW TO PAINT CAMPER CABINETS

Materials and Tools

- ▷ Paint (I like Sherwin-Williams Emerald Urethane Trim Enamel, BEHR PREMIUM Cabinet, Door & Trim Enamel, and BEHR ULTRA SCUFF DEFENSE.)
- ▷ Primer (I like Zinsser B-I-N Advanced Synthetic Shellac Primer.)
- ▷ Flood Floetrol Latex Paint Additive (optional)
- ▷ Varathane Clear Matte Polyurethane
- ▷ Paintbrushes
- ▷ Paint roller kits or paint sprayer (I like Wagner FLEXiO Series sprayers for interior jobs.)
- ▷ Painter's tape
- ▷ Drop cloths or plastic sheeting
- ▷ 220-grit sandpaper
- ▷ Bondo wood filler (as needed)
- ▷ High flexibility painter's caulk (such as DAP Extreme Stretch Sealant)
- ▷ Tack cloth
- ▷ Clean, lint-free cloth
- ▷ Surface cleaner (I use TSP.)
- ▷ Screwdrivers
- ▷ Box wrenches
- ▷ Respirator or mask
- ▷ Safety eyewear
- ▷ Work gloves

Instructions

1. Remove all doors and drawers, labeling each with a piece of painter's tape as to where it belongs. Remove hardware, including handles, hinges, and latches. (I always place them in a baggie and label what they go to for easier reinstallation.)

2. If you're not doing a full interior demo, cover the floor and furniture with drop cloths or plastic sheeting. Tape off all edges of the cabinet base and uppers.

3. For a seamless look, run a bead of paintable caulk along all inside drawer and cabinet door trim seams. DAP Extreme Stretch Sealant is good for this because it has a lot

of flexibility to move with trailer movements. If you're planning on changing hardware, fill the old holes with Bondo wood filler.

4. Clean all the drawers, cabinet bases, and doors thoroughly with TSP, following the package directions, to remove any dirt, grease, or residue. Let the surface dry completely.

5. Scuff the drawers, cabinet bases, and doors lightly with 220-grit sandpaper to create a good surface for paint adhesion. Work lightly to avoid damaging the veneer. A sanding block will be best for this.

6. Clean the surface with TSP once more to remove any remaining sanding dust. Let it dry completely.

7   **8**   **11**   **13**

7. Tape off any area that shouldn't be painted, such as trim, windows, or adjacent walls, using painter's tape. This will ensure clean, straight paint lines. This is especially important if you are using a paint sprayer.

8. Priming is an absolute must to ensure the bonding of your paint. The primers I listed earlier help paint adhere better to the laminate and can prevent stains from bleeding through. Follow the manufacturer's instructions for the specific primer you choose. I highly recommend the Zinsser B-I-N Advanced Synthetic Shellac Primer. Technically, you are not required to sand when using this primer, but I prefer to be safe than sorry. Apply one coat of primer and allow it to dry for the period listed on the manufacturer's label, normally twenty-four hours. Lightly sand with a 220-grit sanding block and wipe clean.

9. If you're painting by hand, cut in around the edges of the trim with an angled brush. Paint the flat surfaces with a high-density foam roller. (Adding Flood Floetrol Latex Paint Additive to your paint will cut down the visibility of brush strokes when painting by hand.)

10. Apply a second coat for even coverage. Allow the paint to dry between coats, following the manufacturer's recommended drying times. Stay out of the camper for at least twenty-four hours to allow the paint to cure and the fumes to dissipate.

11. Once dry, paint the inside of the cabinet doors.

    Optional: Create a faux wood look using the Rustoleum glaze technique I did here. Load the tips of a bristle brush with a small amount of paint and paint the surface in one direction to mimic wood grain. It takes so long to dry that you will have plenty of time to achieve the look you're after even if you mess up at first. To prepare for this technique, prime the cabinets with white or cream.

12. Carefully remove the painter's tape around the cabinet bases while the paint is still slightly wet to prevent peeling off paint. Inspect the walls for any imperfections or missed spots and touch up as needed.

13. For added protection, I apply Varathane Clear Matte Water-Based Polyurethane to all cabinet doors and drawers. Brush on a thin, even coat with a paintbrush. Let dry for two hours and lightly sand with a 600-grit sanding block. Clean and reapply two more coats in the same fashion.

1970 Ideal kitchen before renovation

1970 Ideal kitchen after renovation

1974 Ideal kitchen after renovation

1974 Ideal kitchen before renovation

14. Once everything is completely dry, reattach all hinges and hardware. (If adding new hardware, drill the holes.) Labels on the drawers and cabinets will help put your RV cabinets back together.

Exterior Painting

Your vintage camper will need paint updates on the camper's interior and the exterior. Over the years, the exterior may lose its luster. Or, if you are like Chad and me, you find a gem rotting away in a field, sitting under old oak trees, and the exterior requires a lot of love to shine again.

If you are looking to give your retro rig a fresh new look, a new coat of paint can work wonders. Although to get to the steps of painting, you have a lot of prep work that needs to be done for this paint job to not look like an amateur did it. Lucky for you, Chad and I have had a ton of success with our method, and I will break down the paint type, sheen, and prep we do to get our campers ready to hit the open road in style.

One thing to keep in mind is that vintage campers are made with aluminum siding. Newer model rigs are made with fiberglass siding, so some of these steps should not be performed on fiberglass siding, such as pressure washing. Although RVs might seem sturdy, their siding is quite thin and prone to warping, denting, or even breaking if it's put under too much pressure, therefore you run the risk of damaging it if you use a pressure washer.

When it comes to sheen on the exterior of your camper, you want to go with a high gloss to mimic an actual automotive paint job. This will make for a much more professional look. If you go with a matte finish, it will appear as if it has lost its luster before even having a chance to shine. Trust me on this!

Painted exterior of our RV "Archie"

HOW TO PAINT THE EXTERIOR OF A CAMPER

Materials and Tools

▷ **Paint (I like Sherwin-Williams Everlast Exterior Paint & Primer.)**

▷ **Primer (I use Speedokote Epoxy DTM Primer/ Sealer or Kirker Automotive finishes ENDURO PRIME DTM Epoxy Primer.)**

▷ **Paint sprayer (I use a Wagner Control Pro 130 Power Tank for exterior jobs.)**

▷ **Painter's tape**

▷ **Butyl tape**

▷ **Hex screws**

▷ **Power drill and bits**

▷ **Adhesive remover wheel (optional)**

▷ **Utility knife**

▷ **Self-leveling lap sealant**

▷ **Plastic sheeting**

▷ **Angle grinder and stripping disc**

▷ **Pressure washer**

▷ **Orbital sander**

▷ **Sanding discs**

▷ **Aluminum tape**

▷ **Exterior advanced paintable silicone caulk**

▷ **Screwdrivers**

▷ **Respirator or approved paint mask**

▷ **Safety eyewear**

▷ **Latex gloves**

Instructions

1. Start by pressure washing the entire camper. This is the only time I pressure wash our campers because doing it regularly can damage the siding. Chad and I now like to complete the exterior renovations because it lets us locate any areas that are not sealed properly and may be leaking. This is much easier for us to fix with demo still going on inside rather than waiting until the end and having to run the risk of tearing out interior renovations already completed.

2. The metal trim pieces on the exterior of vintage campers are fastened with metal hex screws and butyl tape (refer to chapter 2 for more detailed information on repairs). Replacing the butyl tape and screws may seem scary, but it is easy and essential to reseal areas around the trailer top edges and windows. Caulk the trim, windows, siding joints, and corner joints with exterior paintable silicone caulk (labeled as flexible). Seal roof seams and vents with self-leveling lap sealant.

3. Scuff the trailer's exterior surfaces with an orbital sander using 80-grit sandpaper (the surface must be rough for the primer to adhere). Follow up with a fine grit sandpaper to smooth out any raised rough spots. Remove faded decals with an adhesive remover wheel drill attachment or, the solution I prefer, an angle grinder equipped with a stripping disc. These discs make decal removal on an aluminum exterior a walk in the park. Another option is a heat gun, but this is very tedious and honestly the grinder is the way to go. Use a clean cloth to wipe down the entire surface after sanding.

4. Remove all the clearance and taillights and tape the wires so they don't fall into the wall cavity. Remove the license plate, door handles, screens (label each for easier reinstallation), and awnings.

5. Use painter's tape and plastic to tape off all the windows, leaving the window frame exposed so that the epoxy primer will coat the frame too. Use a utility knife to cut excess tape from the corners of the windows. If you are not replacing the tires, cover them as well.

7. Paint the camper using the same technique. We use exterior-grade house paint. You can have it tinted in any shade you desire. Using house paint is a great option because it is formulated to stand up to the elements and provides an additional layer of protection against water infiltration. Spray the paint on in light, even coats. It will usually require two coats, depending on the color you choose (darker colors may take more coats for uniform coverage).

6. Prime the exterior on a calm, windless day using a paint sprayer. The primers I listed are two-part mixtures; once mixed, they must be used quickly. Mix the epoxy primer and catalyst together and load the paint sprayer. Spray in an even side-to-side motion, applying a light coat. Repeat if needed, thirty minutes after the first coat.

9. I find it is easiest to add a stripe or accent color by hand because it is way less prep. Tape off any design you want and using the same exterior grade paint in the color of your choice, brush or roll it on with a 3-inch (7.6 cm) paintbrush or ⅜-inch (10 mm) nap roller. Remove the tape when the paint is still wet.

10. Reattach all the handles, license plate, awnings, and lights. I prefer to use new fasteners and apply a bead of clear exterior silicone around the lights for extra protection.

8. Carefully remove the painter's tape from the windows while the paint is still slightly wet to prevent peeling the paint off. Inspect the walls for any imperfections or missed spots and touch up as needed.

1974 Ideal exterior after renovation

1970 Ideal exterior before renovation

1970 Ideal front awning before renovation

1974 Ideal exterior before renovation

1970 Ideal front awning after renovation

1970 Ideal exterior after renovation

wall design

———

When I initially walk into an RV, nine times out of ten
I know right away certain design features that I envision
for the space. If it doesn't happen upon my initial visit,
odds are we won't take the plunge and will just walk away.
Wall treatments are always part of this vision, whether it is
a board and batten, wallpaper, wood accents, or painting
technique. These features add so much character to these
small spaces. Many times, I turn to wall treatments when
I have accidentally damaged walls while demo'ing or
even making repairs to the window frames.

Needless to say, it's something that gives me comfort knowing that if I really mess something up, I can always "fix" it with a wall treatment. For example, during my very first RV renovation, I went a little crazy and tore out an entire wall of closets and some upper cabinets over the main bed. It was my first time figuring everything out, and I happened to break a few areas on the ceiling paneling. I ended up ripping down thin shiplap pieces and making a plaid pattern on the ceiling to cover the nail holes and rips I made.

My favorite thing about DIY renovations is how your mistakes usually force you to be creative and become a focal point that you probably never would have done unless the mistake was made in the first place. Many different wall treatments can be used in RVs that will give you a personalized space and not break the bank. These are lightweight additions that are also very easy for beginners to install.

Ceiling molding used to cover up damage from demo

Molding used to cover demo damage painted white when completed

Painting

Now, I know this may seem like an obvious suggestion, but oftentimes people underestimate what you can achieve with just paint. There's the standard accent wall with a bold color or simply painting all the walls a brighter color to open up a space. Let's take it to the next level! You can do this with a few different painting techniques, such as color blocking, monochromatic painting effects, ombre, faux wallpaper, or even a faux lime-washing technique.

When it comes to most campers, especially vintage ones, the inside is usually dark and brown. Painting the interior a light color is a super easy way to brighten up the space and create an inviting area. So many have their opinions about white paint, but there's a reason it's used so often. Contrary to popular belief, white paint can be kept clean, and it lays

Interior after painting a white base

a perfect foundation for many different design styles to build off.

If you want to step it up a notch, you can try a couple very simple painting techniques, such as color blocking and going monochromatic with paint. Painting a chair rail is where you can use painter's tape to section off the bottom 3 feet (91.4 cm) of the wall to paint it a separate color. Many times, this technique

Interior before painting
a white base

Before painting bunk beds in
vintage camper

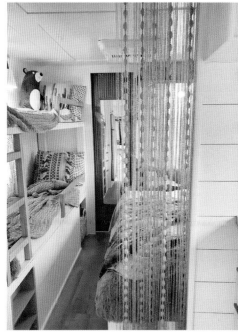

After painting bunk beds in
a vintage camper

Color blocking

Monochromatic design

Painted chair rail

Ombre technique

is also trimmed out with a piece of molding across the line between paint colors, but this is not necessary. Color blocking is similar but can be done in different patterns and use multiple colors for a bolder effect.

The last of the simpler painting techniques would be to create a monochromatic look. This is where you not only paint the walls a color but also the trim and the doors. It's as if the paint just threw up everywhere—but in a very classy and chic way! This is commonly seen in upscale areas, modern designs, and even art deco. You can use a monochromatic look if you want to be bold yet classy, and this can easily be achieved with way less painter's tape to boot!

If you want to challenge yourself, you can try an ombre effect or limewashing technique. Ombre is where you will stay in one color family and start with a darker color on one side and work it into lighter shades of that same color. I find the easiest way of achieving this is to get three or four shades of a similar color and divide the space into equal parts. Paint those few shades from lightest to darkest, and then blend the colors together evenly between each. Don't forget that it's just paint! You can't mess it up because even if you do, it's easily fixed by adding a little more of whichever color is needed to get the perfect blend. If all else fails, you can always paint it back to the original solid color, but I encourage you to try to let yourself get creative.

Limewash has become more and more popular and is commonly done inside stick-and-brick homes. It almost gives a light and airy cloudlike look to your wall but can be done in a plethora of colors. It is a perfect addition to a Mediterranean, modern, or old-world design. Many different companies have products to help create luxurious looks with limewash.

To create a limewash, you start with a base color of your choice that you want to do this technique on. The best colors are earth or muddy tones in a matte finish because this is supposed to mimic a natural finish. Next, you will either get the color just above or below the base color you chose on the paint swatch. (Basically, the same color but a shade or two lighter or darker than the base.) You need a wide bristle brush at least 6 inches wide (15.2 cm) and a paint tray. Simultaneously, pour both colors in the tray one on each side so they meet in the middle. Dip the tip of the brush in the middle, so it has one color on each side of the brush and wipe excess off. The neat part is you just randomly do light strokes all over the wall! It is as if you are trying to wipe all the excess paint off the brush in broad random strokes that eventually create this beautiful blend of the two colors. The key is to use minimal paint at a time and keep blending. As you step back, you will see the result come to life.

Lastly, you can easily create a feature wall using paint to create a wallpaper look. Getting a stencil is an obvious one, but you can also

Limewash technique

Painted wallpaper design

get a sponge and use it to cut out shapes or create imperfect lines for an easy faux wallpaper look. If you have a knack for drawing, you can create small flowers or shapes, or you can mimic a simple wallpaper you may love by just using paint. Many geometric shapes are easily created or swirls and stars—the options are only as limited as your imagination! Inspiration is everywhere, so don't be afraid to step out of your comfort zone and try something new because it's *just paint*.

Wallpaper

Say you don't have an artistic hand, or you see a beautiful mural that would be just the showstopper you want. Wallpaper is a great option. Wallpaper also comes in many textures, giving you more options for a distinctive look.

When considering wallpaper, you have a few different options. You can hang wallpaper by gluing it onto the wall or use a peel-and-stick wallpaper. If you decide to go the peel-and-stick route, you want to keep in mind that if you live in a climate with really big temperature fluctuations, you may have issues with shrinking or pulling away. You also may want to consider choosing a vinyl wallpaper, which makes cleaning very easy; this can even act as a backsplash in a bathroom or kitchen area. The biggest takeaway is that if you choose to install wallpaper, be sure to start the first panel on a level line and have the design seams meet up perfectly. Otherwise, it will be an eyesore rather than a beautiful statement piece.

RV bathroom before renovation

RV bathroom after renovation with vinyl wallpaper

Board and Batten

This technique is such a perfect wall treatment to keep in your back pocket during your camper demo. I have used board-and-batten wall treatment as a way of fixing the destruction I have made when repairing window frames that had rot in them. The great part is that it is completely customizable to whatever size you need. The general look is a chair rail about one third to two thirds the way up your wall with wood trim (battens) spaced evenly throughout the bottom section. So, if you have a seam you need to cover up, you can measure out your battens so they will fall on the seam, and it will be as if it never happened! Optional additions can include adding pegs to the top rail to act as a coat hook or adding another wood treatment, such as a pole wrap in the divided sections or even as an additional border above the top rail. Another way to give a more traditional look would be to add a decorative trim molding to the inside of the battens to give a more upscale look. Once again, you are only limited to your imagination!

Board-and-batten wall treatment

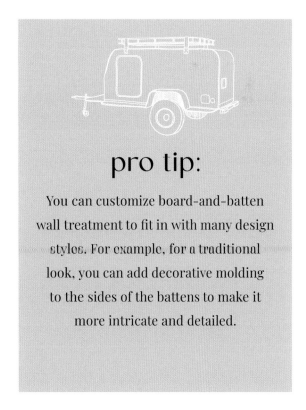

pro tip:

You can customize board-and-batten wall treatment to fit in with many design styles. For example, for a traditional look, you can add decorative molding to the sides of the battens to make it more intricate and detailed.

HOW TO CREATE A BOARD-AND-BATTEN WALL

Materials and Tools

- ▷ 1 × 4s (2.5 × 10.2 cm) (It can be whatever width you prefer, as long as it is 1 inch [2.5 cm] thick.)
- ▷ High-density fiberboard (HDF), also called hardboard (optional)
- ▷ Torpedo level
- ▷ Paint (eggshell or semigloss finish)
- ▷ Primer
- ▷ Silicone caulk
- ▷ 220-grit sandpaper
- ▷ Nail gun
- ▷ 1" (2.5 cm) brad nails
- ▷ Liquid Nails construction adhesive
- ▷ Bondo wood filler
- ▷ Tape measure
- ▷ Calculator

To know the amount of supplies you need, figure out how far apart you want the battens (vertical 1 × 4s [2.5 × 10.2 cm]). To do this, use the following calculation:

- ▷ **Entire length of wall divided by desired spacing (commonly 16 to 18 inches [40.6 to 45.7 cm])**
- ▷ **That number multiplied by the actual batten width (a 1 × 4 [2.5 × 10.2 cm] batten is 3.5 inches [8.9 cm] wide)**
- ▷ **Total wall length minus the total width of all battens (2nd calculation)**
- ▷ **That number divided by number of spaces (1 less than your first calculation)**

Example:

- ▷ Wall length **187 inches** (475 cm) divided by 17-inch (43.2 cm) batten spacing = 11, so **11** battens will be needed.
- ▷ 1 × 4 (2.5 × 10.2 cm) battens at 3.5 inches (8.9 cm) wide, so 3.5 × 11 (8.9 × 27.9 cm) = **38.5** inches (97.8 cm)
- ▷ Wall length 187 inches (475 cm) – batten widths 38.5 inches (97.8 cm) = **148.5** (377.2 cm) inches
- ▷ Last calculation 148.5 inches (377.2 cm) / one less than total battens needed 10 = **14.85** inches (37.7 cm)
- ▷ **Spacing between each batten placement is 14.85 inches (37.7 cm). Whew!!**

Instructions

1. Attach HDF, if needed, to cover up a large area. Apply a continuous bead of construction adhesive across the back and nail the HDF in place. This will give you a smooth finish with no texture, which is what you want for the finished look. Just be sure that if you use it, a batten will cover any seam.

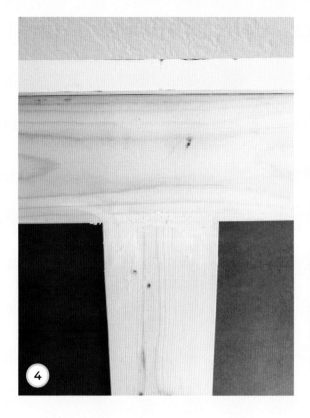

2. Decide how far up the wall you want the board-and-batten section to go (it typically runs one-third to two-thirds the way up the wall). Measure and mark the top horizontal rail. Position it and check for level with a torpedo level. Attach it by spreading a continuous bead of construction adhesive on the back and nailing it in place with brad nails.

3. Measure and mark the batten spacing. Cut the battens to fit between the top rail and the floor. Attach them with construction adhesive and brad nails as you did the top rail.

4. Fill the butt joints where the battens meet the top rail with Bondo wood filler. This will make the seam disappear so it looks like one piece. Sand the wood filler flush after it dries. Apply a bead of silicone caulk along the vertical seams.

5. Prime and paint the surface. I use eggshell or semigloss paint for easy cleaning but less shine.

Shiplap

I don't care what anybody says, shiplap is not a fad! I love the ease and impact this simple wall feature can have. I think it's a great way to add a blank canvas that still has a little bit of character. Big-box stores have premade ship-lap boards, but they are pretty thick and can add unnecessary weight. I buy very thin luan or melamine in 4 × 8 (1.2 × 2.4 m) sheets and rip them down into 6-inch (15.2 cm)-wide boards. Not only are these much lighter, but they are also much more economical. You can get eight 8-foot (2.4-m) shiplap boards from one sheet that costs about $20 USD, compared to the price of one premade shiplap board that runs about $9 USD.

Another great thing about shiplap is that you can add it everywhere or in just certain areas as a feature. Since they are smaller boards, it makes more intricate cuts easier to tackle as you would only be dealing with 6 inches (15.2 cm) of wood at a time. This style goes well in a farmhouse, boho, or coastal design but can easily be made to look more masculine if painted in a deep moody color. When installing these shiplap boards, you also need to decide on the spacing you want to have between them. I use a nickel gap space between each board when securing them. To secure, you can use Liquid Nails construction adhesive and brad nails fastened at alternating angles to ensure they grab.

Once everything is secured, you can achieve a finished look by running a bead of caulk in the corners. Because there is a gap between the boards, a trick to removing the caulk out of those gaps is to use a flat head screwdriver to pry it out.

✈ Shiplap accent wall

Microcement

Another method to create visual interest is to use a product called microcement. This is an extremely thin layer of fine cement that gets applied the same way as joint compound when skim coating a wall, but it is very durable. The risk of cracking on seams is possible, but I stick to each panel individually separated by a wood accent beam or moulding piece. Microcement also comes in the finish color of your choice, so once applied, it is the final look. This is a perfect addition to a Mediterranean or modern look and can give a very upscale feel to the space. Just like everything beautiful, it comes with sacrifice as this is a process to apply. Yet, it is worth the look! Microcement comes in a few different brands, but I will discuss the one I have experience with: Smartcret.

HOW TO COAT A WALL WITH MICROCEMENT

Materials and Tools

- ▷ Metal trowel
- ▷ Microfiber roller
- ▷ Paint tray and roller frame
- ▷ 40-grit, 220-grit, and 400-grit sandpapers
- ▷ Steel spatula
- ▷ Masking tape or wide painter's tape
- ▷ 6mm plastic sheeting
- ▷ Smartcret Smart Primer Grip nonabsorbent primer
- ▷ Smartcret Base Microcement
- ▷ Smartcret Smart Liso in the pigment of your choice
- ▷ Smartcret Smart Varnish

Instructions

1. Tape off the surface you'll be coating. Microcement dries the same as cement does, so you want to be sure to cover anything nearby with plastic sheeting. Clean the wall area so it is free of dirt and debris. Let it dry completely.

2. Shake the Smart Primer well before pouring in the tray. Roll on the primer using light pressure. It's clear, has the same consistency as water, and dries in thirty minutes. This application is essential to ensure the microcement bonds to the wall.

3. Use the metal spatula to mix the Smart Base Microcement well. Spread it on the wall in a thin layer with the metal trowel. Smooth out the surface as best you can. Experiment with different pressures to see what works best, and after a few strokes, you'll get the hang of it!

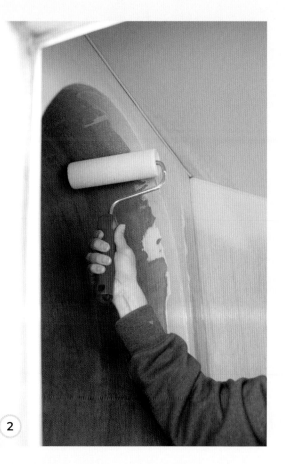

2

4. After the first coat dries for six hours, hand sand the entire surface with 40-grit sandpaper. It will look worse but will feel much smoother. Wipe off the dust and apply the second coat the same way you did in step 3. Let it dry as before and sand again with 40-grit sandpaper.

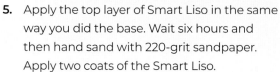

3

5

5. Apply the top layer of Smart Liso in the same way you did the base. Wait six hours and then hand sand with 220-grit sandpaper. Apply two coats of the Smart Liso.

6. Let the surface cure for twenty-four hours and then roll on the Smart Varnish. Apply three coats in one day, leaving two to four hours for drying between each coat. Sand the surface after the first and second coats with 400-grit sandpaper.

7. Remove the tape and plastic sheeting and stand back to admire your new accent wall.

6

Arches

A unique way to add architectural interest inside your RV is to create arches. This can go well with many different design styles such as modern, industrial, or Mediterranean. Depending on the depth of your opening, this look can be achieved fairly easily. I recently did this and covered them in a microcement to give a very organic look to my design. It's also a huge statement that is rarely seen inside these tiny homes on wheels and will surely stand out. If you already have a square opening, the below tutorial will guide you in creating an arch for your space. It is also possible to cut out an arched opening within a wall, and you can follow this tutorial to complete that.

Large closet turned into an arched opening

HOW TO BUILD AN ARCHED OPENING

Materials and Tools

- ▷ ¾" (19 mm) plywood
- ▷ 1 × 2s (2.5 × 5.1 cm)
- ▷ ⅛" (3 mm) utility board
- ▷ Jigsaw
- ▷ 1½" (38 mm) wood screws
- ▷ Power drill and bits
- ▷ Crown stapler and staples
- ▷ Medium-grit sandpaper
- ▷ Wood glue
- ▷ Bondo wood filler
- ▷ String
- ▷ Pencil
- ▷ Tape measure

Instructions

1. Measure the width of the existing opening and cut a square piece of ¾-inch (19 mm) plywood to that size. Measure and mark the center of one side of the plywood square. Add ½ inch (13 mm) to that distance and measure down from the edge center point. Drive a screw partway at this point and tie a string tightly to it. Hold a pencil ½ inch (13 mm) down from the edge of the square and tie the free end of the string around the pencil. Use this string compass to draw an arc from one side to the other of the square.

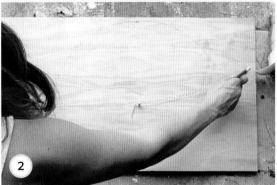

2. Cut this marked arc out with a jigsaw, cutting on the waste side of the line. Use the cut arc as a template to mark and cut a second plywood square.

3. How deep of an arch you want will determine how long you need to make your 1 × 2 (2.5 × 5.1 cm) braces that will go between the two plywood cutouts. Measure the depth and subtract 1½ inches (38 mm) (the thickness of both sheets of plywood). Cut at least eight braces to this length. Glue the braces in place between the two upper corners using wood glue and secure using 1½-inch (38 mm) wood screws. Attach the remaining braces evenly spaced along the arch. This becomes the structure that will go into the opening.

4. Screw the arch in place in the opening with 2½-inch (64 mm) wood screws, making sure it is flush with the front of the opening. Rip a strip of the ⅛-inch (3 mm) utility board to a width that matches the depth of the arch. (If your arch is narrow, you may need to mist water on this board and slowly pre-bend it before installing. This will prevent it from cracking.) Cover the arch bottom with

the strip, stapling it to the 1 × 2 (2.5 × 5.1 cm) braces with a crown stapler. If any given area of the utility board bows away from the arch, secure it in place with a small ½-inch (13 mm) screw.

5. Coat the seams of the arch with Bondo wood filler. I use wood filler because it is much more elastic than wood putty, which would crack. Sand down the wood filler and either paint the arch or coat it in microcement following the process I described on page 118. Microcement gives your arch that adobe look and is a durable finish.

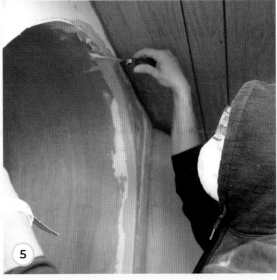

WOOD ACCENTS

Even though most campers are built with wood as the main focal point and it may seem like all I want to do is get rid of it, it really is not the full picture. I mean, when the walls, ceiling, cabinets, floors and sometimes even lighting is brown faux, then yes, I do want to brighten it up a bit! My favorite thing to do after painting everything a fresh light color is to add wood accents back in but in a more impactful way. A few of my favorite wood accents are faux wood beams or corbels, butcher-block countertops, new luxury vinyl planking, or narrow cedar planks on a ceiling or wall space.

When it comes to faux beams, you may be thinking that it's a crazy idea, but it adds such a unique and unexpected touch to your space. Adding butcher-block countertops allows you to bring in an array of different wood tones that also serve a very functional purpose as well.

In my latest travel trailer renovation, I distressed 2 × 3s (5.1 × 7.6 cm) and created a wood beam with corbels in the front window along with faux hollow beams across the ceiling to contrast against the stone look on the walls that had microcement.

Bringing in these natural elements can make for a luxurious and organic space. I have added faux beams in a toy hauler that I renovated into a masculine lounge, and it really made it come to life, bringing in the rich wood tones up against a black ceiling. Each build will be different depending on how much weight you remove; the amount of weight you remove will guide you in knowing how much weight you can add back in. Creating hollow beams from pine is usually what I do to keep them light. The cedar planking I use on ceilings is extremely lightweight as well. I discuss these methods in detail in chapter 4 when giving information about ceiling modification options.

Wood corbel framing front window

➤ Wood banister with intricate trim as a dinette backrest

EXTERIOR

So much focus is always placed on the interior decor, but do not forget to show love to the outside beyond a new paint job. When Chad and I completed our first exterior paint job on a 1974 Ideal travel trailer, it came out amazing. Yet as I looked at the fresh coat of white paint and new running lights, something was missing. From the get-go, I knew I wanted to cover the front folding awning with wood slats laid out in a geometric pattern to liven it up. This can be done with cedar lattice boards as they are thin, lightweight, and meant to be outdoors. I glued them directly on the original slats and stained them in a rich color to pop. This has become something I tend to do to these vintage awnings as it is such a unique look that really adds a homey touch.

Even after that first trailer had the awning completed, it still was missing something. I decided to add a lattice wood trim around each window frame, and that was just what it needed to break up all the white paint. Again, I did this to the latest RV we renovated, and it makes all the difference. To secure the lattice, you cut the pieces to size and push them up against the window frame. The lattice is

Wood lattice added to the front awning

Wood lattice added to the exterior frames of the windows

Cedar planks on the back frame of the trailer

Small cedar flower box on the back storage area of the trailer

soft wood, so an imprint of the screws can be made. Then, you drill a hole where there is a screw imprint at both ends of each piece where it meets the corners of the windows. Remove the screw that holds the window in place and replace with a slightly longer screw that goes in through the lattice and then into the window frame. Add a bit of silicone, and they'll stay secure.

Lastly, if you have a back area that extends on your trailer, you can utilize it as a back porch. On the back end of the 1968 Prowler, there was about a 20-inch (50.8 cm) bump out on the frame that did not have a purpose really. I decided to add cedar planks to create a deck so we could store wood, bikes, and so on, during travel. In true *me* fashion, I could not stop there and added a small little fence to one side along with a flower box to give so much character to this girl's caboose! The point is don't be afraid to try new things and experiment with what you can. If you are conscious of how much weight you are adding, don't be limited to what already has been done. If you have an idea, figure out how to make it happen because where there is a will there is a way! It's not just a saying for nothing.

backsplashes and showers

———

There are so many different options available when it comes to backsplashes and shower surrounds, some of which may seem unconventional to most. With a few modifications during installation, you'll have endless options to make your personality shine through in your space. The design world has come very far with offering realistic products, some that even mimic stone yet keep it lightweight. I like to think that many of these options are some of the biggest accents that can be easily attained in your rig. Many can be completed as a weekend project. Throughout this chapter, I will go through different options I have found to be successful when updating backsplashes and showers along with step-by-step guides.

Backsplashes

A fun way to add a pop of color or design is to incorporate a backsplash in the kitchen or bathroom. There are so many different options to choose from, and depending on the size of the space, you can even opt to use real tile! This is a great way to really expand on the design style you choose for your space. Adding a patterned Spanish tile or stacked stone can really aid in the design, making your space much more unique. So many products exist now that range from beginner to advanced regarding installation, including, paint, wallpaper, peel-and-stick tile, and even real tile. When dealing with smaller areas such as a kitchen backsplash, you usually can afford to use real tile because the amount needed for the small space will not be too heavy or expensive.

PEEL-AND-STICK TILE

Peel-and-stick tile has come a long way. Some brands can easily be mistaken for real tile, and they come in so many different patterns, materials, and sizes that you can usually find one that will fit within any design style. I have used many different brands and styles throughout my renovations, and peel-and-stick tile is an amazing lightweight and beginner-friendly option that can be done in a day. Most come in sheets where multiple tiles are imprinted on a 12 × 12-inch (30.5 × 30.5 cm) sheet, but some bigger patterns come as individual tiles. I used a white hexagonal tile in my boho trailer renovation, and it has lasted perfectly for the past four years.

Hexagon peel-and-stick tile in RV kitchen

Faux slate peel-and-stick tile in toy hauler renovation

Faux stone peel-and-stick tile in van conversion

My number one tip when installing this type of tile is to start on a straight line and be consistent with lining the grout lines up. Even the slightest inconsistency will be drastic when you stand back, especially so with hexagonal and subway tiles. One of my favorite products is a peel-and-stick stacked stone tile that comes in a 6 × 24-inch (15.2 × 61 cm) panel. The awesome thing about it is that it's made from actual thin slices of real stone, making it feel and look extremely authentic. I have used the dark stone in a dark and moody renovation I did along with the lighter version for a soft boho look in our van conversion.

Real ceramic tile install in vintage RV kitchen

REAL TILE

You may think I am crazy, but I promise you real tile can be used in an RV! You must make some considerations due to the weight it will add, but if you have the available weight to spare, it opens an entire plethora of designs you can do. When installing, you can make a few alterations to ensure a long-lasting application.

Materials and Tools

- ▷ Tiles
- ▷ Tile saw or cutter
- ▷ Silicone caulk (in the color you want for your "grout")
- ▷ Caulk gun
- ▷ OSI Quad Solvent Caulk (which I use as an adhesive)
- ▷ Tile spacers
- ▷ Tape measure
- ▷ Sharpie
- ▷ Baby wipes
- ▷ Bondo wood filler
- ▷ 220-grit sandpaper (optional)
- ▷ Ear protection
- ▷ Safety eyewear

Instructions

1. Ensure the surface on which the tiles will be installed is completely clean and dry. Fix any damaged area (you can use Bondo wood filler to fill any holes or seams where repairs are made). Sand the dried wood filler smoothly for a level or plumb surface. Dry lay the first row of tiles and adjust so you have at least one-third of a tile on both ends.

2. Level the camper and make sure the countertop is level. Start the first course of tiles at the counter (you will work up from there) by marking a level line to follow in placing the tiles. Apply a bead of OSI Quad Solvent Caulk to the back of a tile and press it firmly in place against the wall. This adhesive sticks fairly quickly, so only a few seconds of good pressure should suffice.

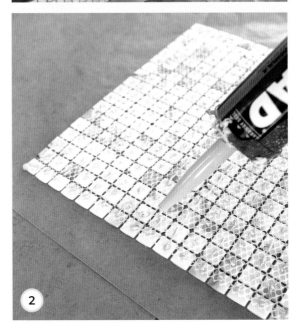

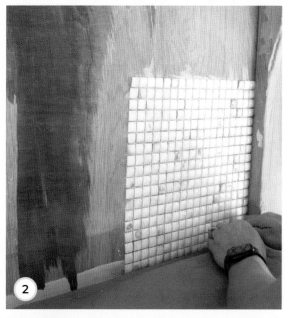

Continue this process along the bottom of the backsplash, adding ⅛-inch (3 mm) spacers between each tile.

3. To cut end tiles to fit, carefully mark and then cut the tile on a tile saw with a diamond tip blade. (A tile saw is a combination of miter saw and table saw, with water splashing on the blade to keep it cool.) Always wear ear protection and safety eyewear when using a tile saw. Dry the cut tiles before applying the adhesive.

4. Let the adhesive dry overnight and then remove the spacers. Instead of grout, I use flexible silicone caulk. The movement in campers and RVs can easily crack standard tile grout. Use a caulk gun and a tube of silicone caulk to lay a bead between all the tiles. Wipe the tiles clean with a baby wipe, being careful not to pull any silicone out of the joints. Once complete, let dry and you are done.

Alternative Backsplash Options

SHIPLAP: When covering the main walls of your RV, you can continue using the shiplap throughout the backsplash. It will make for a clean and unified space that can fit within many different design styles. Using ripped down strips of thin luan, you can add spacers between and paint it any color. They can be stacked horizontally to elongate a space or installed vertically to give more height to the space and draw your eye up.

Shiplap backsplash

TIN: Another lightweight option is to use tin ceiling tiles. They easily can be glued to your backsplash and even carried up to the ceiling if you want a dramatic look. They can be bought in a variety of finishes, such as copper, gold, silver, black, or shabby chic for example. Tin is perfect for an industrial, glam, or traditional look, depending on the finish you go with.

Tin tiles

Herringbone wood design

WOOD: The options with lumber are endless. You can find very thin strips in a variety of wood types premade or even rip down small pieces to create patterns and designs. I have even used paint stir sticks to make a herringbone pattern. You can play with different stain colors to achieve a repeating pattern within the wood as well. Another creative idea is to cut thin blocks off a 4 × 4 (10.2 × 10.2 cm) at different depths to glue next to each other to construct a backsplash with visual and tactile depth.

PAINT AND STENCILS: A very beginner-friendly option is to simply paint your backsplash a contrasting color—better yet paint a pattern. People often get intimidated by using a bold color or attempting to create a design, but here is a little secret: It's just paint! You can easily get rid of it if you hate it. A bridge between paint and wallpaper is to stencil a wallpaper. So many different patterns are available and can be customized with any colors you choose.

Showers

When it comes to showers and bathtubs in your RV, I always want to try to save what is there. It is a very daunting task to correctly place a shower pan or new tub. If the existing is in good shape, there are many ways to bring new life to it. The easiest and best way to revamp an old tub or shower is with a paint specially formulated to be used in these spaces. This is a super beginner-friendly way to brighten up those dingy spaces without having any demo. I have had great success with Rustoleum appliance epoxy paint for this. I have never chosen to use real tile in the shower purely because the weight it would add to most vintage RVs would be too great. However in newer rigs that have a higher GVWR, tile definitely can be used and make for a show-stopping space. Other options are using a variety of FRP or vinyl sheeting.

PVC faux stone panels in vintage RV

PVC PANELS

Another fun option is to use PVC panels. I always love to search for something new, and I have come across a few different types of PVC panels that I have made work in a shower. We all know that PVC is waterproof, but these are so lightweight and thin that they can easily be installed over the existing shower walls. The ones I have found usually come in 2 × 3-foot (61 × 91.4 cm) sheets, so the most crucial part is ensuring they have good adhesion and that the seams where they overlap are siliconed to seal them. A few I have found were the black medallion pressed one below and more recently the stone veneer shower. To make this panel appear more stonelike, I added a waterproof putty product from DAP throughout all the grout lines (even the ones in the middle of the panels so that it looked more realistic).

➻ PVC black panels for RV shower

SHIPLAP SHOWER

I wanted so badly to figure out how I could get a shiplap shower that looked seamless with the rest of one of my trailer renovations that had shiplap throughout. I came up with a plan that has worked out so well and was very cost effective! At big-box hardware stores, you can find an outdoor-grade plywood that is very thin and on one side is a glossy smooth finish. This finish is a waterproofing. I bought a few boards and ripped them down into 6-inch (15.2 cm) strips, just as I do when making any other shiplap. The only difference besides the type of plywood to get are the steps to install it. Use a waterproof membrane such as RedGard or TANK/10 and apply it to the whole shower's interior. It's a very thick paint that will dry rubbery and create a water-proof membrane. Once dry, I take my boards and apply the same waterproofing membrane to the backs (rougher side) and edges of each board as I secure them to the wall. Use brad nails to hold the boards in place, and once the RedGard dries, it will act as a glue. Instead of wood filler, use silicone to fill the nail holes and then paint with an exterior-grade house paint in a high gloss.

WALLPAPER

Wallpaper comes in both peel-and-stick as well as glue-on. Depending on the pattern, you can really change the look and mood of a space with wallpaper. A few things to note is that climate shifts can affect wallpaper. That is not to say that it cannot be done! With proper application, you can create an amazing fea-ture wall or accent piece in your space. For this tutorial, I will explain how to install peel-and-stick wallpaper that is a vinyl material, which is why I was able to do this in a shower.

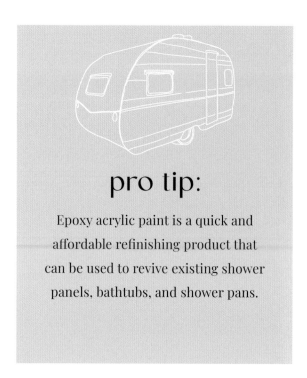

pro tip:

Epoxy acrylic paint is a quick and affordable refinishing product that can be used to revive existing shower panels, bathtubs, and shower pans.

VINYL SHEETING

Vinyl sheeting is a great alternative for shower surrounds in these small spaces. These vinyl sheets are a flooring material but serve as a waterproof membrane perfect for showers. The reason these are gaining popularity is because they have prints that resemble tile in a much more design-forward and modern style than in the past. The process to install is straightforward. You measure the entire interior of the shower and cut a piece of vinyl slightly longer, about 6 inches (15.2 cm). Using a vinyl sheet adhesive, you coat the entire shower walls with it and smooth the vinyl sheet out over it. Remove air bubbles, trim the edges, and add a small PVC trim. This is a great way to easily change the look of your shower or even a backsplash.

↠ Shiplap shower

HOW TO INSTALL PEEL-AND-STICK WALLPAPER IN A CAMPER

Materials and Tools

- ▷ Peel-and-stick wallpaper
- ▷ Level
- ▷ Tape measure
- ▷ Rubber squeegee or plastic putty knife
- ▷ Sharp craft knife
- ▷ Tack cloth
- ▷ Surface cleaner (I use TSP.)
- ▷ Pencil

Instructions

1. Remove obstructions from the surface to be papered, including trim pieces and switch or outlet covers. Clean the surface with a tack cloth and cleaner and let it dry completely.

2. Ensure the camper or RV is level. Measure out from one side ½-inch (1.3 cm) shorter than the distance of the wallpaper panel width. Draw a level line there to have a plumb line to keep your first panel straight. Cut a panel to the length needed, adding a few inches (8 to 10 cm) so you have some wiggle room.

3. Line up the first wallpaper panel with its edge against the plumb line. Pull a small portion of the backing off at a time, smoothing out the wallpaper toward the edge. Do this in small sections and use a squeegee or putty knife to remove air bubbles as you go.

4. Once the panel is completely secured in place, cut away any excess at the top and bottom and along the side if it is an edge piece.

5. Continue hanging subsequent panels in the same way, being careful to match the pattern panel to panel. This may require adjusting the starting point on a panel, depending on the pattern you have chosen.

Optional: If you are only applying wallpaper to a section of a wall, I would add a trim piece just the same as if you were tiling. This could be if you are trying to define a dinette area from a couch area. They share the same wall. Additionally, for any vinyl wallpaper you may use in a shower, I would recommend a PVC trim that is siliconed at the seams and corners to ensure it remains waterproof.

countertops and kitchen accessories

An anchoring piece of the design will be your countertops. You want to make sure they are lightweight, durable, and above all show-stoppingly beautiful! The more counter space available the better, and so many options are out there to take this key design element to the next level. I normally choose to continue the same countertops throughout the entire RV to keep a cohesive look throughout such a small space. However, it is definitely possible to mix it up and have a few surfaces that go well together. Whether you want a high-end-looking laminate, customizable epoxy counters to mimic stones, or even butcher block, the amount of options available within each to tailor to your design aesthetic is vast. So, let's dive into the world of countertops!

Countertops

When you get an RV, nine times out of ten you will have laminate countertops. Now, laminate has come a long way since first being used. Many laminates today mimic beautiful stone. Yet, with renovations, especially with vintage trailers, many times you want to upgrade the appliances and must make alterations to the existing counters. When I do renovations, I always change out or update the counters in the kitchens and bathroom.

When securing new countertops, I always use Liquid Nails. It's a simple way to get great adhesion to the cabinet bases. I will walk you through some affordable and lightweight options—some that will look and feel as if they are real stone!

LAMINATE

Most vintage campers and even newer model RVs come with laminate countertops. I know I said I always change out laminate counters and often use laminate counters that mimic the look of granite, marble, corian, or wood. These countertops are easily installed and cut down to fit your desired size. Another benefit is they are durable and affordable, making them a great option for your camper.

CONTACT PAPER

A very budget-friendly option is to use contact paper. This option may not be for everyone, but it is an option that is simple to do and will make a significant impact. So many different prints and color options are available that you really can get creative with the design. The downfall with this option is that it is not as durable as other materials and may lift with extreme temperature changes.

METALS

Another option for countertops is to install thin sheets of metal. This can be quite pricey depending on the material you choose, but it makes for an amazing look. These countertops are perfect for an industrial or moody vibe. Stainless steel or copper are a few metal countertops that can be quite unique.

Samples of laminate countertop options

Stainless steel countertop

Butcher-block countertops

BUTCHER BLOCK

I love bringing natural elements into my designs. One of my favorite countertops to use is butcher block. Not only does it have a beautiful look, but it also can serve multiple purposes to prep your food on. You can find different varieties that are hollow, with the outer edge and top being a thin butcher block to cut down on weight. You can choose from a variety of finishes and wood types or even stain and seal the wood to your own color choice. Another excellent quality of butcher-block countertops is that if they do become dingy or damaged at all, you can simply sand them down and reseal to make them brand new again!

EPOXY

Epoxy countertops are one of my favorites of all. The creative and custom looks you can craft with epoxy are endless. Epoxy is clear, so you can tint it any color by using something as simple as spray paint. If you can think it, you can make it with epoxy. I have created dark granite

Butcher-block countertops

counters, white marble-looking counters, and stone edges using this technique. Epoxy is inexpensive and looks high-end. If protected correctly, it is exceptionally durable, and it allows you to have a custom stone look that is very lightweight. Many different companies offer epoxy, and after pouring my fair share, I will walk you through the steps to create your own, with a few tips and tricks to help you with this DIY project.

HOW TO POUR AN EPOXY COUNTERTOP

Materials and Tools

- ▷ Medium-density fiberboard (MDF) (optional)
- ▷ Epoxy
- ▷ Spray paint (one or multiple colors depending on the look you are going for)
- ▷ Z Counterform metallic powders in assorted colors
- ▷ Mixing buckets (large and small)
- ▷ Power drill and mixing attachment
- ▷ Orbital sander
- ▷ Brad nails (optional)
- ▷ 220-grit sandpaper discs
- ▷ 400-, 600-, and 800-grit sanding blocks
- ▷ Paint stir sticks
- ▷ Squeegee
- ▷ Small paintbrushes (optional)
- ▷ Bondo wood filler
- ▷ Wood glue (optional)
- ▷ Putty knife
- ▷ Heat gun or torch
- ▷ Level
- ▷ Sheet plastic or builder's paper
- ▷ Masking tape
- ▷ Tape measure
- ▷ Respirator
- ▷ Safety goggles
- ▷ Work gloves

Instructions

1. Measure the depth and width of the countertop and multiply those numbers to get the square footage. Use this number to purchase the correct amount of epoxy. I always add at least 10 percent extra to ensure you do not come up short. Epoxy is messy! Protect surrounding surfaces with taped down sheet plastic or builder's paper.

2. Depending on whether you have changed the existing countertops, you may need to make some repairs. (If you are just updating existing counters, you can pour epoxy directly onto them.) I always have major repairs, so I create a new substrate. Rip down a sheet of ¼ to ¾-inch (6 to 19 mm) MDF to the desired depth of your counter (standard RV counters are between 18 inches and 24 inches [45.7 and 61 cm] deep). I usually plan for a 24-inch (61 cm)-deep counter because counter space is precious!

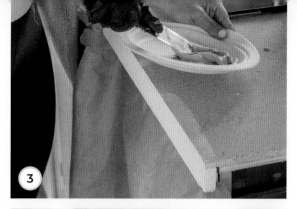

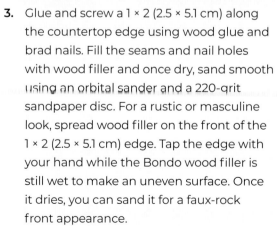

3. Glue and screw a 1 × 2 (2.5 × 5.1 cm) along the countertop edge using wood glue and brad nails. Fill the seams and nail holes with wood filler and once dry, sand smooth using an orbital sander and a 220-grit sandpaper disc. For a rustic or masculine look, spread wood filler on the front of the 1 × 2 (2.5 × 5.1 cm) edge. Tap the edge with your hand while the Bondo wood filler is still wet to make an uneven surface. Once it dries, you can sand it for a faux-rock front appearance.

4. Prime the substrate. Depending on the look you want, paint the entire substrate the base color. So, if you want soapstone, paint the base black. If you desire marble, paint the base white.

5. Check the level again. Epoxy is self-leveling, so it will run toward gravity. The camper should be perfectly level, or you should pour the counters outside where you can ensure level.

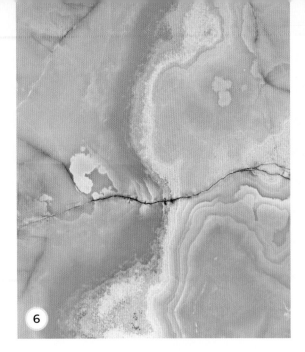

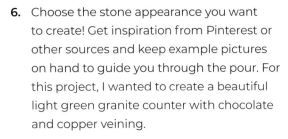

6. Choose the stone appearance you want to create! Get inspiration from Pinterest or other sources and keep example pictures on hand to guide you through the pour. For this project, I wanted to create a beautiful light green granite counter with chocolate and copper veining.

7. Once you choose your look, gather supplies. For this project, I needed the epoxy base, cream pigment, light green spray paint, and bronze, brown, and black metallic powders from Z Counterform to create the veining. Make sure you have one small mixing bucket for each color of epoxy you will need, along with a large container to combine the colors if necessary.

8. Measure the amount of resin you will need for the square footage you're covering in a large bucket. Add the hardener and mix with a drill and a mixer attachment.

Note: As soon as you mix these, the clock starts ticking. You have time, but the mixture will eventually begin to harden. Mix the epoxy only when you are ready to pour.

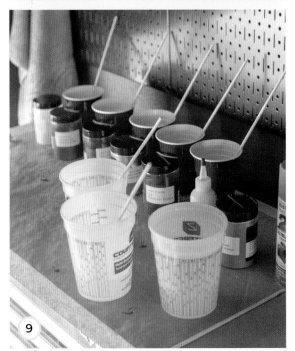

9. After mixing, divide the epoxy into smaller containers. If you are using a certain color only for veining, a cup or so should suffice. To create a granite or "swirly" base look with multiple colors, you may need more separated out into individual containers. (I used multiple small containers for different veining, along with three larger ones for the base pigments.)

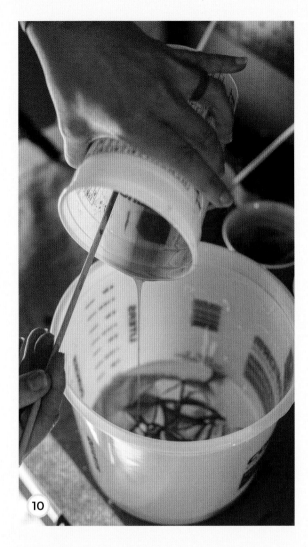

10. Once all the colors are separately mixed, alternate pouring larger amounts of base colors back into the larger container.

11. This next part is the fun. Pour in a linear fashion, in a circular way, or in just a completely random pattern (if you are creating a granite look). However, if you want a solid base color, just pour out the epoxy mixture and spread it with a squeegee. Whatever you choose, you really cannot mess this part up, nor can you control it!

12. Epoxy naturally will flow and level out with gravity. I try to stay away from the edges at first and ensure the entire counter is covered and then pour close to the edges. Once it starts leveling out, the edges might have had some areas missed. You can use a roller or paintbrush to make sure they are evenly coated. I usually wait about fifteen to twenty minutes after the pour so that the epoxy is a little thicker and does not run off as quickly.

13. Adding veining is where you get creative! Having an inspiration picture on hand will be helpful to keep you on track with your desired look. The sooner you place veins, the larger they become in the finished countertop. This is because as epoxy hardens, the veining will not be able to spread as much. That said, you may want to add veins at different times. To make the veins, dip the edge of a paint stir stick in the colored epoxy and run it across the counter in a smooth fashion, allowing epoxy to run off the smaller tip. The quicker you move, the smaller the vein; if you move slower, it will give the epoxy time to run off and create larger veins. After about thirty minutes, do smaller veining that will not bleed as much and will stay small. Another

tip is to take a small edge of either a craft paintbrush or putty knife and lightly dab at your veins. You also can also drag them out slightly to look more natural.

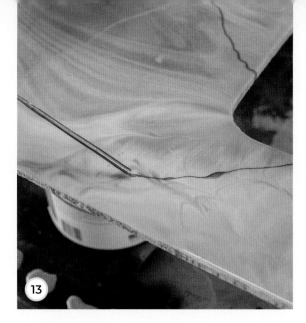

13

14

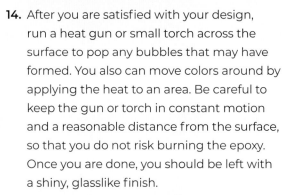

14. After you are satisfied with your design, run a heat gun or small torch across the surface to pop any bubbles that may have formed. You also can move colors around by applying the heat to an area. Be careful to keep the gun or torch in constant motion and a reasonable distance from the surface, so that you do not risk burning the epoxy. Once you are done, you should be left with a shiny, glasslike finish.

15. After about two hours—once there are no drips coming off the sides—run a paint stick or something flat across the bottom of the counter. The epoxy should be tough but still pliable enough to remove any drip marks so that you have a smooth bottom ledge.

16. Let the epoxy cure for twenty-four to forty-eight hours until it is completely dry and hard. At this point, you are finished, although you can go one step further for a matte or honed stone look. Sand down the epoxy surface with a high-grit wet sanding block. Start with 400-grit sandpaper, working to 600- and finally 800-grit. Wet the sanding blocks and lightly sand the entire surface with each. Finally, clean up any residue and remove the tape and plastic sheeting.

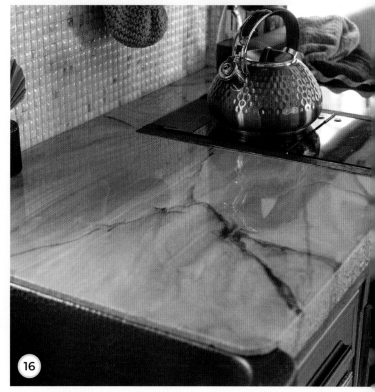

16

Kitchen Accessories

The kitchen is often called the heart of the home, and that is the same in RVs. Kitchens are always within the main living space of your rig and take up the most square footage in your trailer. I not only look to update the area but also to add as many functions and beauty as possible! I hope this next section will leave you looking at your space in a newfound creative way—to not only improve the aesthetic, but also get the most out of your space in unique and innovative ways.

SHELVING AND DISH DISPLAY

I cannot tell you how many people dislike that I create open shelving in my camper renovations. I know that it's a bit unconventional, but certain things can be done to make it work. I want to show you a few different types of opening shelving that I have found to hold up and be functional.

GUIDE TO BUILDING DISH DISPLAYS

In a few of my trailers, I have found vacant spaces that could be utilized as storage. Most of the time, these happen to be where an older stove was housed or "boob" TVs used to be located. I love blending function with beauty and always going against the grain to create functional additions to existing spaces. By simply measuring the inside height, width, and depth of your open cavity, you can build a hollow box that can slide in its place. Next, using a spade bit, drill holes the size of your preferred dowels. I usually use ¼- to ½-inch (6 to 13 mm) dowels. Drill holes approximately 2 inches (5.1 cm) apart on the front edges at

Floating shelves between cabinets

Floating shelves in arched opening for storage bins

Shelves with brackets

the top and bottom opening of your hollow box you created. Repeat this process for the back of the box. After you secure the box with the dowels into the opening, you add a 1 × 2 (2.5 × 5.1 cm) at the bottom and top to act as a ledge. These create rows for you to slide your plates in, and the 1 × 2 (2.5 × 5.1 cm) front acts as a ledge to prevent them from coming out during travel. This can be completely customized to the size of your plates, and you have different little pockets to store a few cups or whatever you please. The other cavities that you may create just need to have those items stowed in the sink during travel and displayed when you set your rig up. It's not a big deal for someone who loves aesthetics!

Dish storage display

Dish display where old stove used to be

Space-Saving Ideas

We all know that counter space is essential when in the kitchen. After you account for the sink and stovetop, many vintage RVs are left with minimal free space. I have found that having cutting boards that fit over the sink opening is such a huge addition to the workable surface in your kitchen. The same can be done over the stovetop, although I usually choose to have a connected glass cover that covers it when not in use. Another idea is to create a pull out counter that slides in and out similar to a cutting board in a house. This can be done simply by taking a ¾-inch (19 mm) piece of wood in the finish you prefer and attaching a 1 × 2 (2.5 × 5.1 cm) to the front with a knob that matches the rest of your kitchen hardware. I have even used pine 1 × 10s (2.5 × 25.4 cm) to achieve this very inexpensively.

Many times, I have added a rod across the backsplash of the kitchen or hung one under an upper cabinet or lower shelf. You can find different hooks and hanging baskets to have utensils, seasoning, and even fruit to be on display and easily accessible.

Pull out cutting board

Pull out cutting board for added countertop space

Utensil rod

Kitchen caddy for backsplash

Utensil rod for backsplash

Depending on if you are a full-timer or not, many weekend warriors or travel enthusiasts do not need an oven in an RV. Most of the vintage trailers I have renovated have had ovens that didn't work. When removing them, I usually choose to replace them with only a cooktop, which leaves me with a large vacant opening to get creative with. Most of the time I choose to create a dish display that allows our pretty dishes to be on display and easily accessible. This is done by making a box and adding dowels spaced evenly apart to hold the dishes. A little 1 × 2 (2.5 × 5.1 cm) ledge is all that is needed on the bottom to create a lip and prevent them from flying out during travel.

In my most recent renovation, we removed the oven once again, but I really wanted to preserve the vintage look. I created a hollow box to replace the old oven and mounted the oven door on a cabinet front. This allowed me to utilize the area for storage but kept the vintage flare with the stove.

Faux stove door storage where old stove used to be

faucets, fixtures, and hardware

When it comes to simple ways of updating your RV, this is a great chapter. In under an hour, you can revamp an area with one of these simple DIY projects that can really make a place look and feel more like you. Changing out faucets, cabinet hardware, and even lighting can be done in one afternoon. A slew of finishes is available, from chrome to brushed gold to oil-rubbed bronze or matte black—there is an option for anyone! One thing is to keep it cohesive. You can mix metals in small doses, but overall try and stay with the same faucet finishes and carry that through to your hardware and lighting. A few considerations should be made when making these changes, and this chapter will help you through the process!

Faucets

Think of your faucets as your jewelry. You can have them in a variety of different finishes and sheens, such as gold, chrome, or even an aged brass. They can be subdued or be a statement piece that will catch your eye. Whatever you choose, make sure you stay on theme of the design style you prefer. For modern looks, keep them sleek and minimal, whereas in a boho or traditional setting, you can get a more ornate-looking faucet.

When it comes to the kitchen faucets, you should give yourself a taller one that can allow you to push it off to one side so you can utilize the sink space with a cutting board or cover. Counter space is precious, so always keep that in mind. Another must in my book is to have a faucet where the nozzle can pull down to clean your sink easier. Another option is a motion-activated faucet to help conserve water while using it.

In the bathrooms, keep a few things in mind. Get a faucet that fits the type of sink you have. If it is a vessel sink, opt for a taller mounted one. They also have cool bathroom faucets that let you pull the nozzle out too. When you pick your shower faucet, you will notice that most RV showers have an on/off button switch. When I was on the hunt for aesthetically pleasing RV showers, I came up short, but I started turning toward a bidet. Sounds a little odd, but you can get pretty bidet faucets that are easily controlled by holding down the lever, which is perfect for conserving water if boondocking.

Changing out faucets may seem like a daunting task, but with just a few wrenches, it can easily be done.

Kitchen faucet upgrade

Bidet faucet for showerhead

Vintage-inspired shower/tub faucet

Sinks

Most vintage RVs have exceedingly small sinks, usually made of stainless material or coated in porcelain. You can find many lightweight sinks to replace yours from online sources. Many of these are larger and have a ledge to add a cutting board on top. If you have the weight to spare, look at household sinks. If you fancy a farmhouse sink, you can get one—just be conscious of the material as some can be very heavy, such as fireclay. I have used bar sinks as well, which are deeper and smaller. These can be bought in a variety of finishes as well. This has allowed me to still have a good amount of sink space, but having it narrower allows me to gain more counter space.

When it comes to bathroom sinks, you can easily swap them out if needed but another option is to make it a vessel sink. This can add a lot of character or be a perfect option if you want to redesign your countertop and place your sink in a different area or have a different size one altogether.

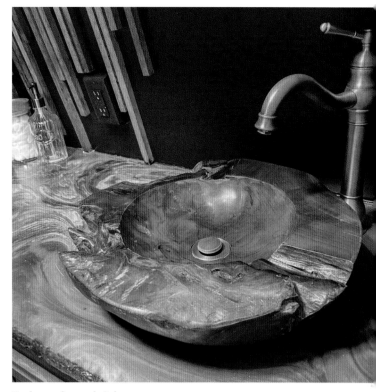

Teak wood vessel sink

Upgraded RV two-basin kitchen sink

Hammered copper farmhouse sink

Cabinet Hardware

HARDWARE CONSIDERATIONS

Just like with anything in an RV, you must always think about weight and movement when it comes to selecting hardware. You also want to make sure your cabinets will stay latched during travel. When I change out my hardware, or build any additional storage, I always make sure to add some sort of closing latch. Every RV, vintage or new, will come with some sort of cabinet hardware latch. It may be magnetic or click in. Depending on if you are changing out your hardware, you can choose to add magnetic closures or double roller catches to the inside rim of your cabinets. Another option is to use actual twist lock hardware that is not only functional but also aesthetic for certain designs styles.

HARDWARE

The variety of knobs and pulls that are available these days is extensive! So, installing new hardware is such a fun way to add character to your RV. From leather-bound pulls, crystals, or rattan moon-shaped knobs, you can find about any design you can dream up. This also is an extremely easy update that really does not require much work. There are many different methods to install hardware, but I will go over the way I do it with a simple tool that can be used for a multitude of hardware sizes and placements.

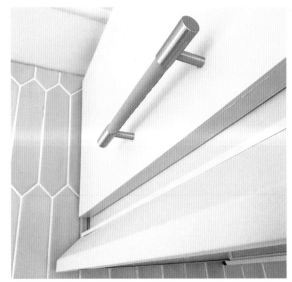
Leather and brass handles

Leather pulls

Cabinet latch hardware

➤➤ Low-profile cabinet hardware

HOW TO INSTALL CABINET HARDWARE

Materials and Tools

- ▷ **Cabinet hardware**
- ▷ **Driver with Phillips bit**
- ▷ **Power drill and bits**
- ▷ **Tape measure**
- ▷ **Pencil**
- ▷ **Template**

Instructions

1. Choose the hardware placement. Center the handles, place them offset to one side, or position them at the bottom of the cabinet. Try out different placements to see what looks best. You can also mix knobs and bar pulls. No placement is written in stone regarding what you should or must do. If you are stumped for a good starting place, line up a knob or the top of a bar handle with the end of a rail (horizontal edge piece) and center them on the stile (vertical edge piece).

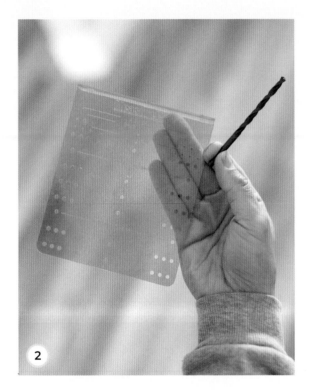

2

2. Determine the center of the drawer and line up with the center of your template. For cabinet doors, measure and mark down in the same distance for every door. Then, line the template up with these marks. Depending on the hole-to-hole distance, find the holes on the template and mark them with a pencil.

3. Use the drill bit for the fasteners that come with your hardware. This is typically a ³⁄₁₆-inch (5 mm) drill bit.

4. Attach the handles by screwing in either side a little bit at a time. Tighten until flush with cabinet door or drawer. If the provided fasteners are too long or too short, buy fasteners in the correct length at your local hardware store. They are common and inexpensive, so don't fret if you run into this issue!

Light Fixtures

With RVs, you will commonly have a mixture of 12-volt lighting and 120-volt lighting. The 12-volt lighting will run off your battery and is useful when dry camping. When you are plugged into shore power, all your lighting—12-volt and 120-volt—will work. Although if you have an inverter and solar power, you will have the ability to be fully powered with your off-grid setup.

If you are wondering which lights are which, you can tell by a few simple checks. First, you can visualize the wires. Any 12-volt lighting will have a black wire and a white wire. Where 120 volts will have both a white and black along with a ground (green or copper wire). The 120-volt wires will also be larger in size than the 12-volt wires, which are small. Another uncomplicated way is to use a voltmeter. If you touch the wires when live with this, it will give you their output.

Although there are differences in these lights, you should know that they can be changed with any light you may find with the proper wiring. This opens a plethora of lighting options that so many do not realize they can include in their designs of RVs! When I found this out, no light was safe from me. When you look at standard RV light replacements, let's just say that you do not have many options, so with this simple trick, you will be illuminating your space with anything you can imagine.

Another thing to keep in mind is that just because RVs move doesn't mean the possibility of a chandelier is out of the question. Many different things can be done to keep movement down during travel, such as using a pool noodle over the down rod or chord to keep a chandelier stiff and lessen the swinging. You can use a bungee cord to secure hanging lights or pendants as well. I also have just removed the bulbs during travel on rope lights—a few extra minutes at setup will not kill you if you want a specific look!

Eight-rope chandelier light

Small crystal chandelier

Chandelier made compatible with an RV

Sconce with on/off button added for use in RV

pro tips:

I prefer to stay consistent with the lighting throughout my design. Find a collection that offers the same style but in different options, such as a sconce, chandelier, and flush mount, so they all are cohesive.

Using a warmer light bulb will give the space a more comfortable, cozy, and relaxing ambiance. I usually shoot for LED bulbs around 3000K.

HOW TO MAKE ANY LIGHT FIXTURE 12V COMPATIBLE

Materials and Tools

- ▷ **Light fixture**
- ▷ **Button switch**
- ▷ **Power drill**
- ▷ **Carbide drill bit**
- ▷ **Wire nuts**

Instructions

1. Choose a flat spot on the light fixture base that can house the push button needed. It needs to be an area that is accessible to drill the hole.

2. Clamp the fixture's base to a work surface and use a carbide bit to drill the hole for the switch.

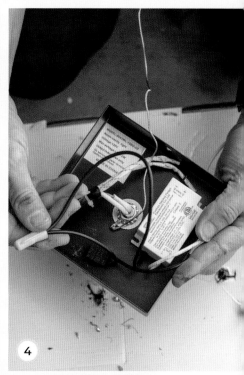

3. Install the button and fasten it in place.

4. The wiring for 12-volt lights includes a black wire and white wire, matching the wires from the camper circuits. Connect the black wire from the fixture to the black wire from the button. Connect the white wire from the switch to the camper's black wire. Connect the white wire from the light fixture to the white wire in the camper. This wiring allows you to turn the light on and off with the switch.

5. Once the fixture is wired, replace the standard bulb with a 12-volt bulb.

seating and sleeping

We all love to travel and camp, but after those long road trips or hiking days, we want to hit the hay in comfort. In many vintage RVs, this can be slightly difficult as many do not have stationary beds, so those comfortable ready-to-go Tempur-Pedic mattresses are a no-go. However, sleeping areas can be quite abundant and functional with the right layout and prep. Getting a really good cushion that can lay the ground for not only everyday living but also convert into a comfy bed is key. The covers are also a huge piece of the design and look. From the material color choices to the thickness and durability of it, this can be customized to your specific needs. Throughout this chapter, I will show you creative ways to get the most out of your space to make sure you will be rested and ready for the day with ample options to accommodate family!

Couches and Pull Out Beds

Unlike a traditional house sofa, travel trailers utilize multifunctional benches that double as pull out beds or even triple as a dining area. This is a huge advantage when you are working with limited space, allowing you to easily modify your daytime seating area into your bedding at night. Additionally, these spaces often have valuable storage underneath the cushions, and this is where you will often find your water tanks and battery banks located.

If you find yourself in a place of needing to replace a couch or even add one into a space, I always look to get a futon couch. This will allow you to easily convert the area into a space for sleeping, cushions included. On top of that, these types of couches are very lightweight and come in a huge array of design styles to match any feng shui.

Velvet-tufted couch pulled out into a bed

Another option is to create a pull out bench. This can be done a couple of different ways. One is using a slat bench, where every other one of the slats pulls out to double the size of the bench, usually forming a twin-size bed. The other option is to add legs on the front of the bench top and have the back portion rest on a ledge when closed. This will let you pull the top out and the feet in the front will be the legs and the back will rest on the front ledge of the bench. This method is an easier build and one that comes standard in many vintage RVs.

Futon couch pulled down into a bed

Slat bench that converts into a bed

Bench seat pulled out into a bed

Dinette area that converts to a bed

Two benches that connect to convert into a bed

Cushions

Many vintage RVs have sleeping arrangements that serve multiple purposes. Because of this, the cushions you choose, especially if you are having to source and replace them, need to be comfortable! Most dinettes and couches that are built into RVs convert into beds. I recommend getting replacement cushions that are at least 4 inches (10.2 cm) thick so that you have enough cushion to be comfortable while sleeping. Another factor when having to replace cushions is to make sure that the height of the back is big enough to fill in the space that pulls out to make the bed. Also, keep in mind if you will need any "filler" cushions. These are the extra cushions that may be needed to fill in gaps while an area is in sleeping position.

When it comes to material choice, evaluate what your plans for the RV will be. Do you have small children? Will you be camping occasionally or living in it full-time? As a family with two small boys, I always get durable material, such as outdoor canvas material or faux leather. This makes for easier cleaning. Having cushions covers that can be removed is a bonus and something I always choose. Zippers that run across the backs of the cushions allow you to throw the cushion covers in the wash, and this option will save you time and peace of mind overall. It can be helpful to add either a grip or hook and loop fasteners to the bottoms and backs of the cushions to keep them in place as well. This won't necessarily be needed for all the cushions, but if you find some that seem to slip frequently, adding a strip of stick-on Velcro or rubber grip tape can help prevent that.

Grip tape under cushions

↠ Bench seat pulled out into a full-size bed

Trailer interior without cushions

Trailer interior with cushions

Having custom cushions made is a pricier option, but one that is worth it. When you look at how much surface area your cushions make up, it is a huge part of not only the RV's comfort but an essential part of the design as well. I had these cushions made from Patio Lane, and they have an insane number of materials, thicknesses, and finishing touches to customize the cushions.

Another option is to either look far and wide on the internet for the correct size cushions or make them. Now, I may be good with my tools, but I am not amazing with my sewing machine—yet when does that stop me? I have only made cushions for one of my trailer renovations, and it was for bunk beds. I took the easier route and glued foam padding to a ¼-inch (6 mm) piece of plywood and wrapped canvas material around it, securing with a

Simple bunk cushion

staple gun on the bottom of the wood. This was a very simple way to affordably make bottom cushions. If you do have a knack for sewing, you can easily find a pattern to create piped cushion covers. This just takes a bit more effort.

Lightweight Headboard Options

One of the simplest ways to add a design element to your bedroom is by creating a focal point with a headboard. This is the same within an RV. The only thing is you need to get creative with the little space you have. Of course, you can always use paint or wallpaper to create an almost weightless feature, but here are a few other options.

BRICK PANELING OR SHIPLAP

You can find faux brick paneling at big-box home improvement stores, and this can easily be added to the wall behind the bed. This paneling can be kept as is or painted any color for a pop of color or a muted look. Another option is to continue the shiplap into the bedroom. A cool option is to create an ombre effect and paint each board a darker shade than the prior. This technique also can be done in a pattern with colors.

BOARD AND BATTEN

We all know the traditional board and batten, but you also can get a little more creative with thin wood inlays in the different sections. I used very thin cedar planks and laid them in a herringbone pattern between the battens. I left the middle sections open to create a focal point to hang art in above the bed. These slight changes created a completely fresh look that was a great statement piece in this RV.

Faux brick paneling

Wood paneling with artwork

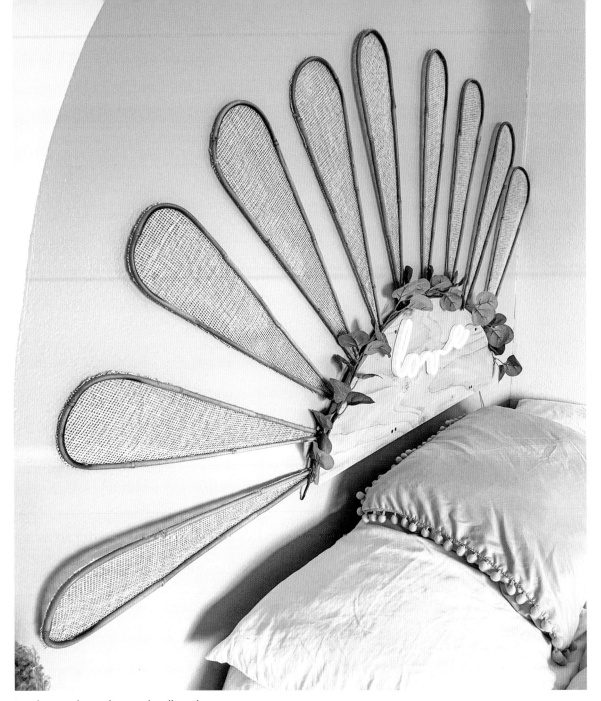

Bamboo garden stakes as a headboard

BAMBOO

Don't forget to look around at materials you normally would not see in design such as bamboo. The lightweight stem is used in gardening as stakes. You can find many different-shaped bamboo trellises that can be tied together to create a unique headboard that's perfect for a boho natural look or even a rustic look. Adding cane can create another dimension to this creation.

Tufted pool noodle headboard

Hanging pillow with leather straps

POOL NOODLES

Have you ever seen those tufted headboards? This can be achieved simply with some material secured to pool noodles! Very affordable and high end looking, this technique will add a soft texture that is perfect to lean up against in bed and can easily be glued and stapled to the back wall. This can work great with many design styles just by choosing unconventional materials. Velvet will go for a more upscale look, where a faux leather or canvas material can work well in a multitude of design styles.

PILLOW AND STRAPS

Another soft and stylish idea is to get a thin cushion or even pillows and take leather strapping to create loops big enough to fit them in. Add a clasp at the top and attach it directly to the wall or hang it with a rod. The straps can be anything you want, not just leather. You even have the option to swap them out for each season if you want to change things up.

Designs That Serve Multiple Purposes

VACANT HIDDEN SPACES

When you have less than 200 square feet (18.6 square meters) of space to live in, you get creative. Finding storage in everything is necessary and honestly kind of fun. Figuring out ways to have something serve multiple purposes is a fantastic way to solve space-saving problems in these little homes on wheels. I always look at the layout of the build and make sure no vacant spaces are left unused. Many times, in newer rigs, hollow cavities will be closed off completely for aesthetic purposes. But being able to access those spots can really help you utilize every square inch. Recently, I renovated a vintage RV where there was a 6-inch (15.4 cm) gap between a closet and the bathroom. Since it was an inner wall, I decided to cut into the space on the bathroom side to enclose it as a storage shelf for soaps, lotions, Q-tips, and so on. This helped keep things off the counters and became an aesthetically pleasing space in the once blank wall.

Bathroom shelf outcove

Store blankets in pillowcases.

Side table storage

THROW PILLOWS

Don't overlook the sneaky storage solution of using throw pillows. You may think it's silly to have throw pillows, but what if you use them to store things? It sounds crazy, but what a perfect place to stuff winter coats or extra linens you may need! I think this solution will appeal to anyone who may live full-time in an RV, as it is always great to have a suitable place to stow away seasonal items or extra items that you may want to bring with you on trips.

COUCHES

Many RVs have dated looking furniture, even in the newly built ones. Not only that, but they also weigh a ton! If you want to change the look of your RV, removing the existing couches

and opting for much lighter and stylish ones will not only update the space but also afford you extra weight that can be added in other places of your design, such as with faux beams or a farmhouse sink.

When choosing a replacement couch, look for those that can transform into a spare bed. This will give you additional space for guests. Many of these futon couches are also on legs, giving you the extra space underneath to utilize as storage.

STORAGE SLOTS

Whenever you change out furniture or spaces in an RV, you usually won't have a perfect fit. Use this to your advantage. For instance, I added in a different couch in the front area of

Vent pipe needing to be disguised

an RV renovation that was about 1 foot (30.5 cm) shorter than the span of the trailer width. I chose to create cubbies on either side of the couch to act as a side table and make it look more built-in. The secret was that the front board I installed was on a swivel, so that it could swing open and be used for storage.

Another example is when I came across the vent pipe for our black tank. It was housed in a full-size wall, floor to ceiling, in our bathroom. Instead of working around it, I removed the wall and only enclosed the small portion that was sticking out away from the exterior wall. It happened to be about the height of the toilet, so I made it into a mini pony wall where we could keep the toilet paper. I always look for ways to open vacant spaces and then turn to design to produce creative solutions that make your space unique.

Wood cover on bottom vent pipe

A Word on Old Appliances

Many times, we have opted to remove old furnaces that no longer work along with old ovens. Now, some might like to cook a turkey or bake cookies on the road, but my family never uses an oven. We will be outside cooking whether we are on the road or at our stick-and-brick house. So, by removing the oven, it frees up a huge amount of space that we can better utilize for us. Always keep your needs in mind, not what the masses may desire because unless you intend on housing them, why should it matter? I turned these areas into dish storage and hidden cabinets.

The other common appliance we remove is the furnace. In these old RVs, the furnace takes up a ton of space and we have never come across one that works. Luckily, we are on the central coast of California with very mild weather and space heaters work fine when you have shore power. This vacant space usually is under the fridge space and can easily be transformed into an additional cabinet, shoe storage, or even a creative tilt-out trash bin, as I did here.

Dish display where old TV was housed

Tilt-out trash can where old furnace was

Dry food storage in open cabinet

Open shelving is one of my favorite additions because it is functional but can serve as a great addition to the decor and aesthetic. Adding a simple trim piece to a vacant opening can turn an empty space into an area like this. We easily have our chips and cereal within reach, but they serve a purpose of looking great too!

things to consider when designing your rv

———

Although many of the normal design changes one can make to a stick-and-brick home can be done in an RV, there definitely are some modifications that need to be made. One of the biggest considerations is to be conscious of the weight you bring in. This is the trickiest part of the renovation process as you may find the perfect piece for your design puzzle but the size or weight of it doesn't allow for it. In this chapter, I will guide you through a few key factors to help your design process within your RV and realize just how possible some of these alterations can be.

GVWR

One of the number one questions I get asked is if my designs affect the weight of the trailer and rightfully so! This is one of the biggest considerations when renovating an RV. First, you need to understand GVWR when purchasing or renovating a camper. This term stands for the gross vehicle weight rating, which tells you what the maximum allowable weight for your trailer's axle is. Every trailer is different, depending on if you have a single or double axel for instance, along with the weight and type of trailer. Vintage RVs typically have a lower rating, whereas toy haulers can hold much more weight. The GVWR is an important number to identify, as it can impact your trailer's integrity, and you can create an unsafe driving condition if your payload is too heavy.

In so many of the vintage RVs I find, they often have portions missing, such as original cushions, tables, or cabinetry. I also am very conscious of how much weight I remove. To do certain design features, I may have to remove something else too. Many times, the original appliances do not work, and I end up replacing them. The older appliances, however, are extremely heavy, which gives me extra wiggle room with what I add back in. Another heavy item is RV furniture, especially the tables and couches. Removing those heavier items gives you so many more options to add more items in if you get a lighter weight piece of furniture to take their place. I normally account for this in my head, but you can absolutely weigh everything you take in and out as well to be sure.

At the end of every renovation, I take the trailer to a weigh station to ensure the RV doesn't exceed its GVWR. You can go to any truck stop or weigh station in your area and ask to weigh your trailer too. You need to take

the trailer off the hitch of your truck so you don't have any of the trailer's weight resting on the tongue connected to your hitch, as this would skew your measurement.

Weighing our 1968 Prowler post-renovations at a weigh station

Construction Material Size

In addition to being aware of the weight of certain items being used, another differentiating feature of an RV compared to a stick-and-brick home is the size of material being used throughout the construction. Many times, it's the depth and thickness of materials where you find the difference.

SCREW LENGTH AND STUDS

Again, with weight in mind, the studs within the walls, cabinets, and benches in an RV are sized down. Most homes are built with 2 × 4 (5.1 × 10.2 cm) studs and even 2 × 6 (5.1 × 15.2 cm) studs, but these are just too heavy for a camper. Your camper needs to use 2 × 2s (5.1 × 5.1 cm) throughout, which decreases the weight dramatically. When needing to make any repairs, be sure to replace studs or add new ones with these same size materials.

That brings us to the next consideration: Make sure to use the correct length screws, ensuring that the two surfaces are attached but not penetrating all the way through your 2 × 2 (5.1 × 5.1 cm). Just because these boards are smaller does not mean your build will be weak.

WALL TYPE

You will not be putting drywall in your camper. Rather, you will utilize a utility board. This is very economical, surprisingly strong, and noticeably light. These boards can be painted, have wallpaper applied, or be adorned with board and batten to stylize your walls. They are approximately ⅛-inch (3 mm) thick, making them simple to cut, even with just a multitool if needed.

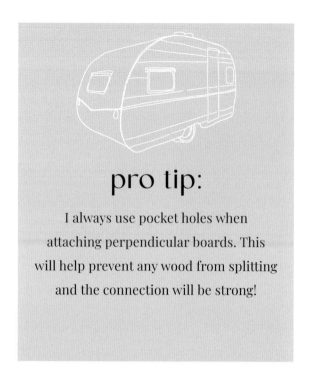

pro tip:

I always use pocket holes when attaching perpendicular boards. This will help prevent any wood from splitting and the connection will be strong!

Climate Plans

We are fortunate enough to live in a place where there's not too much temperature variation. But what if you do? If you are going to live in a cold environment, make sure you can keep warm. I have found that the best way is to utilize a propane furnace. This will allow you to warm up your camper, and propane goes a long way. You always can have a space heater, but if you are not connected to shore power, you better have an exceptionally large battery bank and an inverter that can handle your heater's demand.

If you open any walls due to damage, do not hesitate to add insulation! Most RVs have very minimal thin insulation, especially vintage trailers. Taking the time to properly insulate is something you will not regret.

Another consideration is to have your plumbing winterized. If water freezes in your pipes, it will expand and may rupture your pipes or PEX tubing. An easy fix is to have the ability to drain your system. This is done by having a spout that can be opened near the bottom of your trailer to empty your system. Also helpful is insulating your pipes. You easily can add economical pipe insulation that can not only help keep your pipes from freezing, but also help your water keep its warmth as it travels from your water heater to your faucet.

If you often find yourself in a hot environment, pop an air-conditioning unit on top of your trailer. Again, you will only be able to use it when connected to shore power. One important consideration here is the weight of the AC. Does your trailer's framing support these 50-plus-pound (22.7 kg) appliances? If not, add a metal support on your frame where the AC will be mounted. It is best to do this right after your demolition stage, when the walls can be opened without destroying all your hard work.

We often travel in the warmer seasons.

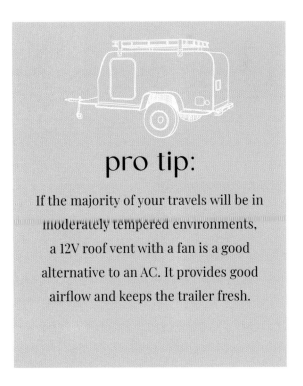

pro tip:

If the majority of your travels will be in moderately tempered environments, a 12V roof vent with a fan is a good alternative to an AC. It provides good airflow and keeps the trailer fresh.

Keeping Decor in Place

If you know me, I love to stage my trailer the moment we set up camp, placing faux trees, hanging pictures, placing candles—the whole nine yards. But some of these items need to be stored appropriately during your travels. I often place items in the sinks during travel, and most of my open shelving will have a lip to prevent plates from rolling away. One amazing product to keep candles, small greenery, or picture frames in place is museum putty or Velcro. I utilize these with my decor all the time, and they help keep things from shifting during travel. Such a simple solution will allow you to decorate more freely in these tiny homes on wheels.

Another trick is for lighting, as I love using chandeliers and other different lighting in my renovations. If you have a chandelier that has a drop down, you can cut a pool noodle the same length and create a slit to slide the chord or rod into which will keep it stiff during travel and prevent it from flying around like a wrecking ball. Another way is to add a bungee cord to tether the light so that it will not sway.

One thing to keep in mind is if you change out the furniture, you need to make sure that it is secure. Many times, if adding a futon, side chair, or stools, have a plan on how you will ensure they do not fly around while driving. I usually build out the futons so they are secure, but you can always add anti-tip or furniture straps that can easily be found at home improvement stores.

Pool noodle to stabilize chandeliers

Museum putty will keep artwork from shifting during travel.

acknowledgments

To Grandpa Rich, a.k.a. "The Blanch Manager," words can't express how thankful we both are to know that we can always fall back on your knowledge if we get into a pickle! You are a jack-of-all-trades and our safety net when we get stuck mid-project. I know we feel comfortable doing many of our projects because we know we can always count on you for advice if we need it.

To our families, especially Vava and Grammie, for always being there to help with our two boys, we are so very blessed to have you all in our lives.

To Thom O'Hearn, our editor and guide throughout the process, thank you for making this endeavor possible. The entire creation of this book has been an amazing learning experience, and we feel like we hit the jackpot on our teacher! Good luck on your next adventure.

Sefra Escobar with Sefra Kay Photography, thank you for always capturing our family the only way you can. I love the attention to detail and in-the-moment shots you are so amazing at freezing in time. Visit sefrakay.photography to book her for wedding or family photography!

Thank you to my DIY girls Paris, Alyssa, Heather, Trisha, Anna, Caitie, Tiffany, Ashley, and Michelle for listening to me vent during my overwhelming days while writing this book. I appreciate the advice and encouragement you guys gave me throughout this experience!

RecPro and Emily Jordan, thank you for taking a chance on us. RecPro has been our supplier for all things travel trailer–related, and Emily facilitated and streamlined everything with ease. They have just about anything you may need to get these projects done. Visit recpro.com to find anything to fix or restore your trailer.

To the many brands that supported us in this last renovation, including Patio Lane cushions, Sinkology, Smartcret, Tile Club, Wagner, Georgia Boot, and Woodgrain.

The following contributed beautiful photos of renovated RVs you'll find in the book.

Nate Kantor and Garrett Foster Green
with Nomadicana
nomadicana.co

Allison Lundeen
@proverbsthirtyonegirl
proverbs31girl.com

Dan Waitkus and Samantha Serfilippi,
the duo behind @rtconversions

Heather McQueen
@forgeandtrek
forgeandtrek.com

Dave and Amelia, the Bay-Browns
@bbandtherv
bbandtherv.com

Brad and Renee Lois with @wisco_flip
WiscoFlip

Elijah & Leann Dixon
@fivetalentshomes
fivetalentshomes.com

about the author

Janelle Payne is the founder of Nailgun Nelly, a blog (and related social media accounts) dedicated to RV/camper and home improvement. Mostly self-taught by fellow DIY creators, Janelle is a firm believer that anyone can tackle DIY projects with power tools. She has a passion for designing on a budget and creating high-impact tutorials and is well known for her transparent videos where she shows the good and the bad that happens behind the scenes when renovating. This daily, realistic experience has led to explosive growth for Nailgun Nelly on social media. Janelle has developed partnerships with dozens of brands, including Wagner, Rust-Oleum, RecPro, and Tile Club, and she has been featured by *Business Insider*, *RV Enthusiast*, *Tiny House Talk*, HGTV Handmade, and more.

index